Rachel Calof's Story

RACHEL CALOF'S STORY

Jewish Homesteader on the Northern Plains

J. SANFORD RIKOON

Volume Editor

INDIANA UNIVERSITY PRESS

Bloomington and Indianapolis

Translated from the Yiddish by Jacob Calof and Molly Shaw

This book is a publication of

Indiana University Press
601 North Morton Street
Bloomington, IN 47404-3797 USA

http://iupress.indiana.edu

Telephone orders 800-842-6796
Fax orders 812-855-7931
Orders by e-mail iuporder@indiana.edu

My Story, by Rachel Bella Calof, © 1995 by Jacob Calof

© 1995 by Indiana University Press

The paper used in this publication meets the minimum requirements of American National Standard for Information Sciences—Permanence of Paper for Printed Library Materials, ANSI Z39.48-1984.

Manufactured in the United States of America

Library of Congress Cataloging-in-Publication Data

Calof, Rachel (Rachel Bella), b. 1876.
    Rachel Calof's story : Jewish homesteader on the Northern Plains / J. Sanford Rikoon, volume editor.
        p.   cm.
    Includes index.
    ISBN 0-253-32942-6. — ISBN 0-253-20986-2 (pbk.)
    1. Calof, Rachel (Rachel Bella), b. 1876. 2. Jews—North Dakota—Biography. 3. Farmers, Jewish—North Dakota—Biography. 4. Jewish women—North Dakota—Biography. I. Rikoon, J. Sanford. II. Title.
F645.J5C353   1995
978.4'004924'0092—dc20
[B]   95-5742
    ISBN-13 978-0-253-32942-4 (cloth) — ISBN-13 978-0-253-20986-3 (pbk.)

11   12   13   14   14   13   12   11

CONTENTS

PREFACE

I approach visits to historical archives with a mixture of hope and trepidation. One of my constant desires is to discover unpublished narratives that give voice to the personal experiences of previous but as yet not widely known episodes of our past. This dream holds especially true when my research focuses on groups that because of race, gender, ethnicity, and class were inadequately profiled in contemporaneous accounts and remain largely ignored in current academic circles. The vast majority of our country's residents unfortunately leave little in the way of self-reflection of their inner lives and everyday events. Scholars have learned to distill complex meanings from available artifacts of the past, but these writings often reveal as much about academic trends as they do the lives of artifact creators. What we often lack is the contemplation and assessment of individuals who not only had to survive but also woke up every morning with their unique sets of doubts, failures, pleasures, and visions.

A few years ago I utilized a Lowenstein-Weiner Postdoctoral Fellowship to search the holdings of the American Jewish Archives (Hebrew Union College, Cincinnati) for evidence of Jewish farming experiences in the American Heartland. I had general knowledge of Jewish farming efforts in the East and of short-lived communalistic ventures scattered throughout the United States between 1880 and 1940. But no publication had ever suggested any significant movement of individual families or any longer-lived settlement areas in the Midwest. To skeptics who questioned my expenditure of time on a project seeming to offer little promise because so few Jews became farmers, I simply replied that I wanted to try to document "both of them." Secretly, I hoped to find proof, or at least indications, of an identifiable movement and some compelling personal documentation of that experience.

Behind the subject heading of "North Dakota" in the American Jewish Archives card catalog I found close to a dozen index cards. The majority referred to records and materials from small congregations and notable families in Grand Forks and other small cities. One card, however, contained the spare notation of a manuscript titled "My Story," the name of Rachel Bella Calof, and an archival collection number. There was no indication of the nature of the manuscript or the date of its composition. I asked to see "My Story" and the first things I noticed promised a great deal—a relatively thick manuscript and the subtitle, "The Early Years—Homesteading," penciled onto the rubber band-bound file folder encasing the text. I opened the folder, and with rising expectations found the manuscript's first lines: "I was born in Russia in the year 1876, and when I was four years old my dear mother died. . . ." I did not know then what lay ahead, but I was immediately captivated by her narrative style. And on that warm spring day in April in Cincinnati, I spent the next four hours mesmerized both by Rachel Calof's telling and by her story.

I leave it to readers of Rachel Bella Calof's narrative to derive their own interpretations of her remarkable personal and physical journeys and her poignant narrative of the internal and external struggles that marked the immigrant experience on the northern plains. Her text comes first in this book because it is her account that speaks most vividly to experience and to the reflexivity that enlightens experience. The two essays following Jacob Calof's epilogue to his mother's story offer further discussion of Jewish settlement in the Heartland and elaborate on her text in the context of the historian's discipline. As you read this remarkable account of "a life worth living," perhaps one piece of commentary that may help light your way is that provided by Rachel Bella's youngest child, Jacob, who prefaced the translation distributed to family members with these words:

PREFACE

We may be powerless to alter what has gone, but we will always be fascinated by the drama of the past and, if we are worthy, will apply its lessons to our present predicaments. If we are fortunate as well, we may discover priceless gifts of pride and confidence in learning that we are products fashioned from excellent material.

A glance over one's shoulder encounters no visible boundary of that which has gone before. We look back to our parents who are the products of their parents. The twentieth century is the product of the nineteenth. New York is descended from ancient Jerusalem, which is in turn descended from Abraham's tents.

We are our past; all of our past. Our personal qualities are not precisely those of our parents. Various influences of earlier generations also season our makeup, in some markedly, more subtly in others.

What older influences helped to mold the characters of Rachel Bella and Abraham Calof are not known, but the quality is unmistakable.

SANDY RIKOON
COLUMBIA, MISSOURI

ACKNOWLEDGMENTS

In 1936 Rachel Bella Kahn Calof purchased a five-by-seven-inch "Clover Leaf Linen" writing tablet and began to reconstruct her life story. Her remarkable journey began sixty years earlier, south of Kiev in the Ukraine. In 1894 she came to the United States to marry a man she had never met, and for the next twenty-three years she lived on a farm north of Devils Lake in rural northeast North Dakota. Her story recounts aspects of her childhood and teenage years in the Old Country but focuses largely on her life between 1894 and 1904 and her experiences on the homestead.

Rachel Bella Calof completed sixty-seven ruled pages of "Jewish" (Yiddish). The appearance of her prose is exceptionally clear and clean, with only an infrequent reconsideration of a choice of words or the insertion of a term or phrase to provide an extra detail or two. She might have made notes before writing in her tablet, but no one in her family ever saw her preparing such prompts. She rarely discussed her past and had no written diary from earlier years. It is as if she had been forming the words in her mind over the years and needed only the time and opportunity to make them come spilling out onto the pages.

We will never know exactly why Rachel Bella Calof took the time and trouble to write her narrative. Certainly there is some internal evidence in her story indicating a desire that her descendants know of her journey and remember this past. That a wider audience might be interested in her narrative was simply not a consideration. In fact, if it were not for the interests and insights of her descendants, this significant documentary and compelling drama might have remained a prized private possession of the Calof family though inaccessible to even family members who could not decipher the Yiddish text.

Around 1980, nearly thirty years after Rachel Bella Calof died, her fourth daughter, Elizabeth Breitbord, resurrected her mother's narrative from a trunk. Determined to make "My Story" available to her family, but unable herself to prepare an English text, Elizabeth Breitbord turned to her brother Jacob Calof, the youngest son of Rachel Bella Calof, and Molly Shaw, who grew up on a farm not far from the Calof homesteads. Molly Shaw translated the Yiddish words and phrases into their closest English equivalents. Jacob Calof then adjusted the translation's grammar and punctuation, relying on his familiarity with his mother's narrative style to maintain the faithfulness of the text to his mother's voice.

There are always difficulties attendant upon translation, and the line between translation and interpretation is always hazy. Particular difficulties accompany the translation of Rachel Bella Calof's Yiddish, which she used throughout her life as her primary spoken language, into written English. In this case we owe a great deal to Jacob Calof, who refused to use outsiders who might have changed any part of his mother's story and who would not have known her "voice" and narrative style. Jacob Calof adhered to the substance, sentiment, and style of his mother's writing as closely as possible. No passages were added or deleted from the original nor were any changes made in the content or chronology of her narrative. Whenever Yiddish terms were not easily translatable into English, the judgment of the original translator and the family's own knowledge of their mother's use of language were the most critical determinants. Rachel Bella sometimes predicted the need to explain a particular term or phrase and included her own definitions, which appear in parentheses in the text. Finally, and appropriately in light of the narrative's multigenerational audience, two of Rachel Bella Calof's granddaughters, Roberta Myers and Johann Smith, joined forces to type the transcription for wider family circulation.

"My Story" eventually came to the attention of a few historical researchers, but it has never been published or made known in any detail. Perhaps reflecting Rachel Bella's own notions of privacy, the Calof family resisted the attempts of writers and others who knew a good story when they read one and wanted to use "My Story" for their own various artistic purposes. More recently, and primarily through the efforts of Jacob Calof, the family has agreed to publication of the full and unaltered translation. We owe a great debt to Jacob Calof and to all other family members for allowing their mother (or grandmother or great-aunt) to speak to a wider audience and for providing supplementary information on the family's history. Most of all, we thank the woman who lived and wrote "My Story," Rachel Bella Kahn Calof, for her voice, her honesty, and her vision.

Rachel Calof's Story

The North Dakota homestead of Rachel Bella and Abraham Calof. Rachel Bella appears in the center, below the handwritten "Mom." Circa 1905.

MY STORY
Rachel Bella Calof

I was born in Russia in the year 1876, and when I was four years old my dear mother died, leaving me a half orphan in company with an older brother, a younger sister, and a baby brother of only eighteen months. My father did not marry again for some time because he wanted to be sure, he said, to select a wife who would be a good stepmother to us children. In the meantime he brought a Jewish servant girl into our home to care for us. This event proved to be a disastrous development for us youngsters; from that day onward, un-yielding misfortune became our lot.

The first initiative of our new supervisor was to reduce the children's food supply, and other requirements for the care of small children were simply ignored. How well I recall the pangs of hunger which attended all my waking hours. Hunger and dirt dominated our young lives. Our overseer gave our food away regularly, but although I knew this I never learned who the lucky recipient was. This sad state of affairs continued for four long years.

When I reached the age of eight, I had already fully assumed the role of protector of my brothers and sister. Now I decided that our lives could no longer continue in this way and I determined to take action. I spoke to my father about the intolerable conditions under which we lived. The servant girl, learning of the trouble I was causing her, beat me mercilessly, but I persisted and continued to appeal to our father upon his return from work as a farmer at that time.

Because of the terrible life that his children were enduring, father made the decision to remarry quickly to provide us all with a better home life, he said. Unfortunately the event of his second marriage marked an even further deterioration of our childhood existence.

My father married a woman with two children, a boy and a girl, both older than us. Our stepmother proved to be a nasty, cruel person with no love or accord for her new husband's children. As the saying goes, "When a father chooses a step-mother for his children, he himself becomes a stepfather." Another old belief is that a husband is more in love with his second wife than his first. In any event our father gave all of his devotion to his new love, to the exclusion of all else.

The new lady of the house quickly took full control of everything and everyone. She assumed absolute power and did with us children as she wished. She punished us continually, without reason and without mercy, beating us daily.

As soon as my father left for his work she would lock the bread away in the cupboard. The best that the household afforded she gave to her own children, and she dealt with us as did Pharaoh with the ancient Jewish slaves. She ordered us to do the heaviest kind of work which required effort beyond the capacity of small children. My eldest brother, then eleven years old, once was forced to lift a heavy load far beyond his physical ability. I recall the incident so vividly. He cried out and fell to the ground in pain so great that he fainted, and when he recovered his senses he complained of stomach pains. I realize now that he probably suffered a hernia. My poor little brother

2

had always been sickly and weak, and unable to further cope with our long-standing pitiful life now spent all his days in bed. And I, now nine years old, sat many hours each day with him, both of us crying forlornly.

My father was always greeted upon his return from his work with complaints about our behavior. My stepmother stated once that my little brother, who was always in pain and pale as death, was getting on her nerves and that consequently her health was affected. My father, I am saddened to say, sympathized with his new love. I went into the bedroom where my little brother lay and I and the other two children sat on his bed and cried inconsolably. My father, goaded by his wife, entered the room and without ado seized my little brother from his bed of pain and beat him without mercy. He bloodied the child who then fainted. My screams reached the heavens. My father declared that he would deal similarly with all of us. We children shook and shivered in shock, and when I saw my brother's blood on the floor, my childish heart turned to stone and I cursed my father with deadly curses.

That evening, huddled around our little brother's bed, we were afraid to cry though our hearts were breaking, fearful that we would invite more abuse if we made any sound. Later my sister and older brother and I were forced to sit at the dinner table while my little brother, also commanded to come to the table, was not able to leave his bed and consequently went without food.

We four orphans occupied one room which contained two beds, one for my brothers and the other for my sister and me. But this night I did not go to bed. I put the two older children in one bed and my sick and beaten brother in the other. I sat beside him and wept bitterly, but silently.

The poor child slept restlessly and when I touched him I realized he was feverish. I dipped a rag in water and applied it

3

to his head. I continued this treatment throughout the night while I silently cursed my stepmother and her children. But most of all I cursed my father from the bottom of my heart.

My little brother was in bed for a week following this incident and then was only able to totter on his feet. From that time he showed no interest in anything. He remained silent and weak and pale. He had no energy and no longer joined his brother and sisters in any activity. My heart broke and tears would come to my eyes just to look at him.

In about a year after their marriage my father and step-mother began to quarrel. One time I overheard her tell my father that she no longer wished to stay with him. Soon after she left with her children, even while my father begged her not to leave him.

Following this happening, our father decided to break up his home and give up his children. His plan was to go to America as soon as he could get rid of us. He proceeded with his plans to dispose of us. I was sent to my paternal grandfa-ther. My older brother was given to my mother's brother who had a sack store and he was immediately put to hard work to earn his keep. My young sister was sent to my mother's sister and was immediately set to work fit for a grown person rather than a little girl. She had developed a stomach ailment and was unable to keep much food down.

My youngest brother, unable to work, found no welcome with any of our relatives and was disposed of to a Talmud Torah, a religious school. He was kept there until his health improved and after a time he was taught there to be a lock-smith. The three children were all in the city of Belaya Tserkov. My new home was in a village called Chvedkifka.[1]

How I longed for my brothers and sister. Occasionally my grandfather would permit me to visit them. It was a long trip, requiring two days for the round-trip, but to see my brothers

4

and sister was worth any hardship. Indeed, it was the most important event in my life. However, at the same time these visits disclosing the hard lot of each of the children, especially that of my little brother dirty and sweaty from his work and always so sad, brought me tears and blood, as the saying goes. His bed was covered with rags for a quilt and the food was bad. This was a charity institution and these were the conditions found in such a place. I would start my visits with such happy anticipation of seeing my poor orphans but would return heartbroken at what was revealed to me.

And so my childhood years passed in tears and suffering. My life was shattered and wasted and I never knew love since I was four years old, except from my little orphans.

I was in my grandfather's house for six years and it wasn't very good for me there. My grandfather was very strict and a religious fanatic. He saw me as a sinful person who required constant watching. I couldn't raise my head up without reproof. He thought I had it too good, and he constantly reminded me of my lowly position while he tried to make life harder for me in the belief, I guess, that it would improve my character.

My grandmother, actually my stepgrandmother, on the other hand was more tolerant and kinder to me than my own grandfather.

At age seventeen I petitioned my grandfather to allow me to seek permission to go to my aunt, my father's sister, who I had heard was rich and, more importantly, lived in the same city as my brothers and sister. I learned that this aunt wanted a maid and I decided that I would ask for the maid's job. If my plan succeeded, I would be independent with my own money while living in the same city as my brothers and sister. With money I would be able to improve their lot.

I arrived at my aunt's house and was given the maid's job. The work was hard. This was truly a palace. It contained eight

rooms and a number of hallways, all of which I was required to wash and wax each day. But the best meals I ever ate were cooked in that house.

I was green at my job. I had never been in a house before that required this kind of care. I tried hard to please my aunt, who was very particular, but within a few months I was doing my work satisfactorily. During this time I was able to see my dear sister and brothers more often than before. Their situations had not improved at all and it was heartbreaking to see how hard their lives were. I was able to help them somewhat but still their condition was bitter. My sister was ill and being treated at a free dispensary, but they were unable to improve her health. My little brother's suffering was heartrending to see. At least, though, I could see them all quite often and help them.

One of my new duties was to buy the meat at the butcher shop. The butcher with whom my aunt traded had a fine, good-looking son. As to myself, at this time, I had heard it said that I was pretty and no fool. The butcher's son often waited on me. He was very gentle and friendly. I used to get a funny feeling inside of me when he was filling the order, but of course I didn't know how he might feel about me. I liked him, I must say, and soon I sensed that he liked me too. I was painfully aware, though, of the danger of developing a friendship with this fine boy. In Russia, at that time, the occupations of butcher, tailor, shoemaker, or musician were considered inferior trades and those engaged in such work were socially unacceptable. Certainly I felt no such distinction as I was of low status myself.

Although I was nothing in the world myself, I was the granddaughter of Eda Velvel Cohen and because of this fact a friendship with this boy was out of the question.[2] It appears that although I was no joy to my relatives, I was capable of bringing them disgrace. A butcher was considered hardly better than a convict, and especially so to my grandfather. Still, we, a boy and a girl, in spite of the disapproval and contempt which others felt for us, were drawn to each other.

The young man was a few years older than I. One day he approached me and asked me to go for a walk with him. I was shocked at such boldness. Yes, I loved him, but I looked at him in bewilderment. I could only believe that he did not know that because of my family I could not associate with him. I thought it best to discourage him as quickly as possible and to not demean him in doing so. I told him that my grandfather lived here and that I was only a visitor in the city. It was a badly conceived lie, for he saw how poorly I was dressed and belatedly I realized that he knew I worked for the wealthy Beolicks. He appeared to take me at my word though, listening politely to my lie, and I returned to my quarters.

As I discovered later, however, the boy fully realized my helplessness and immediately took the initiative. He found out my grandfather's address and wrote him a letter in which he proposed that my grandfather make the necessary inquiries about him. He asked permission to call on me. He said that I was a fine girl and that he was very fond of me and felt that he could bring me happiness. He offered to marry me as I was without a dowry or wardrobe.

I was unaware of my friend's action, but I did know that I loved him and longed for him. Still I knew that I couldn't go walking with him under any circumstances as this would endanger my job and blacken the family name, which in turn would bring terrible consequences down on my head. I was made rudely aware of what was transpiring when my aunt received a letter from my grandfather. Of course he wouldn't even consider writing directly to me. The letter instructed my aunt to take any measures necessary to prevent me from

7

disgracing the family name. He stated that my marriage to a butcher would defame the family name forever.

My aunt summoned me and handed me the letter. This woman was more modern than most people of that time. She did not wear the traditional wig and her children drank milk with meat meals. She would light the samovar on the Sabbath and her children attended public school.[3]

She really looked at many things differently than most women of that age. But although she may have felt some sympathy for me, her main concern was her father and she would do nothing to hurt him. She asked me if I understood everything about this boy. I did not know the meaning of this question but I knew I was blushing for shame and hurt.

My grandfather was still not content with the damage he had done to two young lives. He dispatched a letter to the boy's father telling him not to have hope that he could ever be associated with our family.

I longed for the boy and I know that he yearned for me, but I avoided seeing him again and this episode in my life ended. The butcher boy was my dream and now the dream was over.

So time passed. I reached my eighteenth birthday and my prospects for the future were now very poor. Most girls of eighteen were married in those days,[4] and here I was a servant girl in my aunt's home without resources. I was ashamed of my status as a menial. I had no dowry to enable me to marry anyone of status. My future seemed hopeless.

I secretly hoped that my father had reached America and would send for us children. But this hope was crushed when news was received that the ship in which he had sailed had sunk. I never learned whether he had been saved and I never heard from him again.

Meanwhile God sits above and sees all that happens below,

8

and God finally understood that He had to do something in my behalf. His plan for me was quite complicated.

Another relative of mine, a great-uncle, lived and owned several houses in a distant city. One of his tenants was a girl named Chaya who through a series of amazing events was destined to become my sister-in-law.[5] Chaya had parents and brothers in still another city.[6] Many guests, mostly family members, came to Chaya's house.

She and all of her family were very close to my great-uncle. One of her brothers [Abraham] was in America and had no wife. He had written to Chaya, commissioning her to pick a wife for him and prepare the prospective bride for the passage to America.

Chaya had already decided upon the daughter of the local *shochet* (an authorized slaughterer of animals according to kosher law). The daughter's name was Rachel, as is mine. The arrangement had already been made with Rachel's father, but after further consideration she decided that she didn't want to go to America after all.

My great-uncle was quick to recognize the opportunity of disposing of my embarrassing presence to my relatives and volunteered me as a substitute for the other Rachel. In all justice, he probably felt that this move might also be favorable for my future as well. My great-uncle described to Chaya all my good characteristics and, I am sure, was careful to omit anything detrimental. In short order the decision was made to send me if I was able to pass personal inspection.

I was dispatched to my great-uncle's house where Chaya waited to look me over. What an inspection. She checked me out as one does a horse. Apparently I passed muster because it was decided that my picture should be sent to the boy in America. His name was Abraham [b. July 16, 1872]. He was requested to send his picture in return. After this was accom-

9

plished my great-uncle and Chaya would decide if anything
would come of it.

I hoped that I would be accepted. I realized that I had to take
the chance of going to a stranger in a strange land. No other
avenue was open to me. I was already eighteen years old and
time was against me.

Finally the exchange of pictures was made. I liked his
looks and he wrote that he was pleased with my appearance
as well. I then corresponded with him, and although he
eventually became my husband, the way was neither quick
nor easy.

Chaya now decided to examine me in greater detail. She
said she wanted to know me better and to visit her for the next
Sabbath. I didn't have a proper dress for such an invitation, but
I was anxious to make good and was finally able to borrow a
dress for the occasion. I spent three days under close observa-
tion and undergoing various kinds of testing. As an example,
I was handed a ball of tangled yarn to unravel. I didn't
understand the purpose for this, but I succeeded in unraveling
all the yarn. My future sister-in-law was quite pleased. She
explained that this was a way of testing my patience and good
nature. She said that had I become angry or frustrated in
attempting to unravel the thread I would have lost the opportunity of marrying the boy in America. Thank God I passed all
the tests. God was watching over me and I won Chaya's
approval.

Chaya wrote to Abraham that I was a treasure of a girl and
recommended me to be his wife. In return, my unknown and
unseen fiancé sent me what passed as a passport in those days
of open immigration. It was actually a passage fare and it cost
him twenty-one dollars. This was for steerage passage, which
was the best he could do. He had no money for better
accommodations.[7]

10

The time involved from when I became a servant girl in my aunt's house through loving and losing my butcher boy and preparing for my journey to America was nine months. As the time for my departure approached, my sorrow at leaving my dear brothers and my sick little sister grew. What can one say? We knew that we would probably never see one another again. Words cannot express my anguish at the prospect of leaving them.

My American boyfriend had arranged with an agent in Brescatovaski to plan my journey to the Russian-Polish border. No money had been provided me for the long trip across Russia, Poland, and Germany to Hamburg where I would board the ship to America. I had to raise money for food and other essentials, at least until I reached the ship. This proved to be a tough job. Even though the relatives could well afford it, they showed me no generosity.

Yet it was in their own interests to provide the means to dispose of this troublesome girl who was an embarrassment to them all; a girl, unmarried, already eighteen years old, without a dowry and who might even marry a butcher, thereby soiling the family honor beyond redemption. The reward of getting rid of me permanently won out over their avarice, and they got together fifty dollars which was presented to me with great reluctance.

Many obstacles awaited me during the course of my trip to America, not the least of which was the fact that the passport which I carried was in the name of Rachel Chavetz, the *shochet's* daughter. Prior to my selection as second choice, and when it appeared certain that the Chavetz girl would be the traveler, the husband-to-be had applied to the American immigration authorities and steamship company for passage and admission into the United States for Rachel Chavetz. This was the passport sent to Chaya, and this was the document which I was

11

expected to use for transport to New York and to gain entry to the promised land.

I made my farewell visit to my dear little personal family, my poor brothers and little sister. I was completely broken up. I felt as though my very soul was being torn from my body. Words cannot describe my anguish at our parting.

Our leave-taking was not prolonged. I was instructed to leave immediately for the city where Chaya lived, and which was to be the point of departure for my long journey. Chaya and some of her relatives accompanied me to the train station which was eighteen miles distant. As the train got underway, I was overwhelmed with a complexity of emotions, the most dominant of which was the aching sorrow at leaving my brothers and sister, knowing that in all probability I would never see them again.[8] Fear of the unknown and the uncertainty of my future also occupied my thoughts. I could not even exchange a word with my fellow passengers as I had been repeatedly warned against speaking to strangers. I knew nothing about my final destination. The nature of the lands or the great ocean I would cross were unknown to me. Above all, my welfare was in the hands of a man half a world away, whom I knew only by name and a photographic picture. Who knew what this boy really had in mind. Maybe he intended to lead me into dishonor. God alone knew what awaited me.

I was on that train for three days and nights while my fears and other emotions whirled through my mind. But finally my thoughts settled into a firm resolve that I would face up to my future and do my best to make it a good one. I made up my mind that the boy in America and I shared a common future, and that I would go to him in faith and trust.

I had no baggage except a small parcel which doubled as a pillow. I was hungry and exhausted from my mental turmoil.

Although I had my rubles, I was reluctant to spend any of them for food because Abraham had written that I needed to buy certain supplies before I boarded the ship; things that would help me better survive the sea voyage. I didn't know how much money would be required for this purpose and I elected to keep my little hoard as intact as possible.

Abraham's letter of instruction also informed me that the agent who would meet my train at Brest-Litvosk, at the Russian-Polish border, was named Sarven.

I had been well indoctrinated before my departure with a fear of strangers and the terrible pitfalls which awaited a young girl traveling alone. In view of these dangers, I sent a telegram informing Sarven of my expected time of arrival and instructing him to show me the telegram when he approached me.

Finally I arrived in Brest-Litovsk. I left the train with a good deal of apprehension. Everything seemed so strange. This was a busy place. People were pushing and jostling one another in their hurry. Others were shouting instructions to the newly arrived train passengers to get into taxis. You can be sure that I stayed rooted to the station platform. Three times I was approached by persons, and of each of them I asked his name and to show me a certain telegram. Following these encounters, Mr. Sarven did arrive, identified himself, and showed me the telegram which I had sent him. I stayed at the Sarven home for a week until the agent made the necessary arrangement to transfer me over the border, and I eventually arrived in Hamburg, Germany, without further incident. I was becoming an experienced traveler.

I was forced to wait some time in Hamburg, how long I do not recall, while the ship was prepared for sailing.

As the time neared to board the ship, I became increasingly distraught for I had learned that I faced an ordeal which could result in my being refused permission to board the ship, and thereby left stranded in Hamburg without friend or resources, unable even to return to Russia.

As I mentioned earlier I carried the passport of Rachel Chavetz, the girl whom I replaced for the journey to America. At that time in Europe a travel pass was required for train travel and this pass was in my true name, Rachel Bella Kahn.

Upon my arrival in Hamburg, I was informed by the agent there, to my great consternation, that both the travel pass and the passport had to be presented to gain admission to the ship. The travel agent suggested that I tell the authorities that my travel pass and my money as well had been stolen. Since no other course presented itself, I really had no choice. I had to attempt it.

The fateful day arrived and with a wildly beating heart I presented myself with Rachel Chavetz's passport and my fabricated story to the embarkation authorities, and without ado I was refused permission to board and removed from the line of passengers. The passport would have posed no problem, containing only a name and the country of origin, but the travel pass included a full description of the person to whom it was issued. The authorities depended on this document for identification rather than the passport.

How can I describe my despair. This was, at long last, the dismal end of my struggle for a life worth living. This event occurred in the morning of the day of sailing and the ship which was to carry me to New York, America, would be gone by evening. Utter disaster faced me. There was no way out, and yet at this very moment a special providence was watching over me.

As I stood on the dock sobbing uncontrollably, a man whom I had seen in the steamship office during my desperate attempt to gain admission to the ship approached and spoke kindly to me in German. He beseeched me to stop crying. I didn't know if he was a Jew or not but I sensed immediately that this man was my friend. He asked me to tell him my story and I divulged without hesitation the circumstances which resulted in my passport and travel pass being issued to different names.

This dear man listened quietly to my story and apparently came to the conclusion that I was a decent young lady worth helping. He approached the officials on my behalf and discussed my situation with them while I watched from a distance with my heart in my throat. Then, after what seemed an eternity, he returned carrying a paper for me to sign as Rachel Chavetz. With a happy smile he told me that I would now be permitted to go on board the ship. My exhilaration was boundless. I was so overjoyed that I did not even think to ask my benefactor's name. I thanked him in Jewish [Yiddish] and he understood me. I did not know his name, but I knew he was my angel from heaven.

I had acquired a small basket in Hamburg and this contained my spare wardrobe consisting of a set of underwear, a pair of stockings, and a housedress which I intended to wear when greeting my future husband. Obviously my baggage inspection didn't take long and in a few moments I was on board and assigned my sleeping place.

The bunks were arranged one over another. I chose the highest in the belief that the air would be better there since it was evident that many people would be living in too small a space for the three or four weeks of the crossing. We were on the same deck as the ship's machinery and the din of the engine noises was to assault our ears day and night.

In the two hours before sailing I witnessed many sad farewell scenes. The partings of parents and children were especially poignant. Husbands and wives were taking sorrowful leave of one another, and brothers and sisters clung to each

15

Rachel Bella Kahn around the time of her
engagement to Abraham Calof.

other knowing that in all probability they were seeing each
other for the last time. Their mournful lament reached to the
heavens and the anguish in my own heart was rekindled as I
thought of my own brothers and sister.

We had hardly left sight of land when I became violently
seasick and, unfortunately, remained so for the first twenty
days of the twenty-two-day voyage. My good neighbors in the
steerage carried me to the weather deck each morning and
returned me to my bunk in the evenings.

On the twenty-first day the ship entered calmer waters and
I quickly began to feel better. We were told that we would dock

Abraham Calof around the time of his
engagement to Rachel Bella Kahn.

in New York harbor that evening, but we did not arrive at Ellis
Island until the following day.

In the morning, tense with apprehension and at the same
time anticipation, I dressed in the housedress which I had been
saving for this all-important occasion. Soon my fellow passengers and I were ushered into an enormous room with bars
across the windows which aroused considerable apprehension
because it seemed so like a jail. In short order the various
examinations began which for each immigrant would determine his or her fitness to enter "Heaven." No previous experience aroused for all such anxiety as the test of Ellis Island. With

17

a word or gesture from an official, one standing a few feet from the gate opening to the golden land could be refused entry after having traveled so far. We had to wait until the passengers from a small ship just arrived were herded into the room with us and then examined before anything further happened. Then names began to be called out, and these people passed through the gate to be claimed by excited friends and relatives.

Suddenly I saw my husband-to-be approaching the desk where the officials sat. I recognized him at once from the photograph which he had sent me. Nervously I said to the girl sitting next to me, "There comes my beloved." Everyone around heard me and they all laughed with happiness for me. I wasted no time. Basket in hand, I headed for the gate. The name Rachel Chavetz was called out and I tried to get through, but I was prevented until my friend approached and, recognizing me from the picture which had been provided him, claimed me and led me into the promised land.

We greeted one another in quite a friendly manner and he presented me with a gift of two oranges. Soon we were on a streetcar heading for his living quarters.[9]

I was simply bewildered by the sights and sounds which assailed my senses. Everything was so strange; the immensity of the city, the manner of the people, the houses, the sounds and smells, all confused and astonished me. It was too much to absorb so quickly. By the time we reached Abraham's boarding house I felt weak and tired from the effects of the long sea voyage and the impact of my new surroundings. Even though all the people in the boarding house treated me warmly, I felt a rising tide of panic. I was successful, though, in not revealing my feelings. I was fed and a woman showed me to my bedroom. This turned out to be the dining room cupboard [pantry] with no doors and windows. I learned to my alarm that Abraham's sleeping place was a couch in the adjoining dining room. The landlord slept in another part of the house, and needless to say I felt most uncomfortable with this arrangement, and my alarm deepened. Here I was, rooming with a stranger in a stranger's house, in a strange land where I knew no one. Although everyone had treated me kindly, I was determined to remain very alert. I had no intention of undressing. I lay down on my bed fully clothed and fell into a fitful sleep.

I was suddenly aware of strange company. The room was overrun with a cloud of four-legged creatures and some with even more legs. These visitors, which turned out to be bedbugs and cockroaches, were doing all kinds of tricks and engaging in racing matches. It was unbearably hot in this room which had no windows, and awakening to this mass of bugs surely did not improve my frame of mind.

My boyfriend, lying on his couch in the dining room, was unable to sleep and soon became aware of my dilemma. He lit the dining room lamp and we talked for a time until exhaustion overtook me. It was at this moment that he suggested that I sleep in his bed and that he would be my company. I could have sunk into the earth with shame. All that I had been warned about and had guarded against since I left Russia suddenly came into sharp focus and I prepared to defend myself.

The boy, seeing my distress, immediately apologized. He seemed so sincerely sorry that I recovered some of my poise and decided that I was in no immediate danger. Still I remained uncomfortable and wary. The boy then suggested that I sleep on his couch in the dining room and he would take my bed in the pantry. Before retiring to the dining room, I went to the kitchen for a drink of water. Upon entering the kitchen my attention was drawn to a loaf of white bread on the table so covered with cockroaches as to make it appear like black bread. I took no water and fled back to the dining room. I lay on the couch, fully clothed you may be sure, and tried to put my situation into some sort of perspective. The fear that I had fallen into the very situation against which I had so guarded again plagued me. My suspicions were heightened by the action of the landlord who had left me with a strange boy while he retired to another part of the house. These thoughts pursued me through the long sleepless night. What had become of the bright and wonderful future which I had anticipated the morning of this very day? How terrible things had turned out on my first day in America. What would tomorrow bring?

In the morning, the landlord and his wife, finding me in the boy's bed, greeted me with great hilarity, suspecting the worst. I spoke to them coldly, telling them that I was pleased neither by their implications nor the conditions in their house.

Before leaving for work that morning the boy spoke to the landlord for some time of what I knew not. I began my second day in that alien world with many misgivings but I could not afford the luxury of tears. I felt ill but I forced myself to assess my situation calmly. Even though everything and everyone seemed so strange, including my boyfriend, I felt that the boy was more of a friend to me than any of the other people I had met. I thought about this for some time and decided that probably my future still lay with him. So I rededicated myself to our common cause, and by the time Abraham returned from his work I was indeed glad to see him.

After supper he suggested that we go for a walk. I instinctively resisted this proposal. Although I was determined to try to build a future with Abraham, I meant to do so only if I could be assured that he proved to be a man of acceptable character. As of the moment I was not prepared to trust him fully. Although my great-uncle had spoken favorably about the boy, he had already been in America three years and I suspected that a person's character could change considerably in less time than that in America. Well, I decided to do my share in developing trust between us and so I consented to go for a walk in New York with an almost stranger. Maybe I was changing too.

We walked to a park and sat on a bench. Abraham began to speak to me in a friendly but earnest tone of voice. He said that although he had provided the passport and passage money, I was not to consider myself obligated to him. He said that he could understand my distrust of him, and that if I was unable to believe in him and didn't want him, he would still remain my friend and would help me find employment and thereby be independent of him.

I was so relieved to hear him speak so, and believing now that he was a man of good character I responded that I was satisfied to marry him. We were both happy at the way things turned out. Our affection for each other grew in the following days. When he went off to work I was lonesome for him and I was given to understand that he missed me too. By the time, two weeks later, when we left New York for a great venture, our engagement seemed to have gotten off to a good start.

Abraham's family had come to America three months before my arrival. The family consisted of his father and mother and a younger brother, Moses, who lived with his parents, and an elder brother, Charlie, and his wife, Faga, and their two young children. Two nieces, Doba and Sarah, had also come to the new land to be with their husbands.[10]

All these people had gone on to North Dakota which had become a state five years earlier. They had come to claim homestead land which was now being offered to induce people to settle there. The year was 1894. Abraham was convinced that our best chance to make something of ourselves was to avail ourselves of the offer of the free land. With our mutual

21

effort we would build and prosper. I had to agree. It seemed a godsend to penniless people who could not hope to buy land.

I had no idea where North Dakota was or what the country was like, but I was prepared for the challenge. Of course I had no intimation of the incredible hardships which awaited us there. And so, two weeks after setting foot on the golden *medina* (land) of America, I was on my way to become a pioneer woman and to help build my new country. My life in Russia already seemed remote.

We left the train in the town of Devils Lake, North Dakota. We were met there by Abraham's brother, Charlie, who was to escort us to the area where the family had already filed homestead claims and where we also were to stake our claims. This region was approximately twenty-five miles distant across the trackless prairie.

I felt a sinking feeling when I saw this man. He was quite dirty and badly dressed with rags on his feet in place of shoes. He looked like a subnormal person to me, a suspicion which was confirmed the moment he began to talk. I disliked him instantly and instinctively. I could hardly believe that this man was Abraham's brother. Was he typical of the kind of people I would be associating with in my new life? I must say, upon meeting the other members of the family who had accompanied Charlie, my apprehension appeared to be well-founded.

Included in the group were Abraham's father, younger brother, Moses, and the two nieces, Doba and Sarah. The appearance of these girls was truly shocking. They wore men's shoes and a rough looking garment. Only common peasants wore such clothes in Russia. I was dismayed to see such attire worn by Jewish women. It was indecent. Poor as I had been all my life, I had always worn a dress like any self-respecting Jewish woman. I was highly indignant at the time, but I want

to say now that one of these nieces before long would prove to be a real friend to me.

Charlie had borrowed two horses for the trip across the prairie. None of these people owned a horse. Their livestock consisted of three oxen and three cows which they all shared. We all climbed aboard the wagon and headed for home, not my home but that of one of the nieces. After a long ride across the limitless prairie we arrived there, where I met the remaining adult family member, my future mother-in-law.

As we climbed down from the wagon I looked again at this assembled group and my heart sank still lower. The two brothers were so dirty and unkempt. They had wild unshaven faces. Their skin was broken out in big pimples and they wore rags wrapped around their feet in place of shoes. I learned that the women had no shoes at all but were wearing the men's shoes this day in my honor.

Even this dismal spectacle was inadequate to prepare me for the scene inside the miserable shack which was this woman's home. As we entered my heart turned to ice at what greeted my eyes. This was my first sight of what awaited me as a pioneer woman. The furniture consisted of a bed, a rough table made of wood slats, and two benches. The place was divided up into two sections, the other being the kitchen which held a stove and beside it a heap of dried cow dung. When I inquired about this, I was told that this was the only fuel this household had. They had no firewood at all. What a terrible way to live. I silently vowed that my home would be heated by firewood and that no animal waste would litter my floor. How little I knew. How innocent I was. Shock and deprivation were no strangers in my young life, but seeing what faced us in this new and hostile environment I could hardly choke back my tears of grief. Two children were inside, a girl and a baby boy. The little girl's feet were wrapped in rags. She had never owned a pair of shoes.

23

The women prepared the welcoming supper. Even now, forty-three years later, I well remember that meal which consisted of flat pieces of boiled dough and cheese, with water or milk to drink.

Abraham and I had sat up for three nights on the train and had a jolting ride across twenty-five miles of prairie. I am sure that he also was shocked at what we had experienced this day and was as weary as I. I turned to him and said, "Let's go home." However, our hostess quickly suggested that we sleep there that night. I was puzzled by her suggestion. How could she accommodate so many people in so small a space, holding only one bed? The woman, sensing my unspoken question, explained that she and I would occupy the bed, her husband and Abraham would sleep on straw in one corner, and the children would occupy another corner also piled with straw. I may have only sensed it at the moment, but what I was seeing was probably the greatest hardship of the pioneer life, the terrible crowding of many people into a small space. Lack of money and building material and inadequate fuel supply were the primary causes which forced people to huddle together for warmth and a place inside four walls. Of all the privations I knew as a homesteader, the lack of privacy was the hardest to bear.

After supper the other niece and her husband left for their shanty which I understood was about a mile away.

Before Charlie left he took Abraham aside to bring him up to date on the general condition of the various households. I learned that three shacks even smaller than the one I found myself in had been erected for each of the Calof homesteading families. Abraham's father and mother occupied one. Charlie and his family, including his brother Moses, lived in the second, and the third palace was reserved for Abraham and me. What great news. My rosy future as a pioneer was getting grayer by the minute. Even then I had no idea what dreary prospects would be revealed to me in the following days.

Each of the three shanties was twelve-by-fourteen feet, I was told, with dirt floors. They could be moved from place to place if needed, and in times to come such mobility became necessary. Each shack was located on the land which each family intended to file on as a homestead. The government offered a quarter section of land to any adult who would cultivate the ground. Each quarter consisted of one hundred and sixty acres. The land had to be satisfactorily cultivated within fourteen months; if not, the homesteader, if he wished to remain on the land, had to buy it at one dollar and twenty-five cents per acre. If the government was satisfied with the development of the quarter section, the homesteader would receive title to one hundred and sixty acres at the end of five years. At the end of the five-year period, if it was found that the homesteader had farmed more than the original quarter section, he would have to wait an additional six weeks for title to his one hundred and sixty acres and pay a twenty dollar penalty. Single women were permitted the same homestead rights as men but married women did not have such entitlement. Of course all engaged girls in this territory filed claims before marriage. I will tell you about my own experience in this regard later in my story, but now let us return to the present.

Another piece of information which Charlie had told my husband was as follows. The day before, a heavy wind which was not unusual on these great open plains had first torn the roof off Charlie's shack and then had turned the structure upside down. Although no one was injured they ended up sitting on the roof. Now he and his family were lodged with his parents until the damage could be repaired.

The following morning, leaving the niece's place, Abraham

25

and I headed out across the prairie to our shack. I anxiously looked forward to seeing our own home, however humble. My excitement mounted as we pushed through the shoulder-high prairie grass, but Abraham remained strangely quiet and I was soon to learn the reason for his sober mood. There was no road and after a time I asked if we were close. He did not answer, but in a few moments we broke out of the tall grass into a cleared space, and I beheld the building, twelve-by-fourteen feet as had been earlier described, not only lacking a floor but roofless as well. Just four board walls, sitting in the middle of the trackless prairie. I was unable to speak. Wordlessly, my man led me to his parents' shack. Before we reached there, Abraham broke his silence. He told me that we had no choice but to live with his parents until a roof could be put on our place. He said that a special place had been reserved in his parents' home which would be our own space. I could not understand how this could be so, but I was soon to know. The shocks were coming so quickly that I was becoming numb.

As we approached, my future mother-in-law came out to greet us and ushered us into our separate apartment. I could not believe my eyes. A pit had been scooped out in the center of the dirt floor. This was the private space which we had been promised. Looking about at the people and the space provided for our living, I knew that I was very close to the living level of an animal. As the realization of what I faced grew, my heart turned to stone. There sat Charlie, muddy, tattered and filthy, an appearance shared by his wife and children. His four-year-old boy, cross-eyed with an ever-running nose, wore only a shirt but no pants, while his elderly grandfather was clad only in drawers but also no pants. The shack's furnishings offered no happier view. The single bed was made of rough boards. It had two legs on one side. The other side was hammered to the wall. The table was similarly attached to a wall. The bed had

26

neither spring nor mattress, only a spread of straw covered with a sheet. The floor was earthen.

I was urged to make myself at home. To think that this was to be my home for even a short time brought bitter tears to my eyes. My fiancé, knowing the dread which gripped me, proposed that we go for another walk. Our footsteps brought us back to our roofless future residence. How forlorn and desolate it looked against the limitless prairie. He explained that there was no money to even buy the nails for a roof. With no roof, he pointed out, we had no choice but to stay with his parents for the time being. I was too depressed to respond, and after a bit we continued our tour of the Calof empire to examine Charlie's overturned shack. We then returned to an early supper of groats and milk at the parents' place after which the men would attempt to right Charlie's shack so that he and his family would have a place to bed down that night.

As I looked at the assembled company at the table, the groats stuck in my throat. I began to cough violently while the tears streamed from my eyes. Everyone thought my tears were caused by my choking spell. How wrong they were.

After setting the overturned shack upright, Charlie and family departed. So passed the daylight hours of my second day in the land of opportunity. The coming night was about to add its share of unpleasant events.

At dusk the preparations got under way for going to bed. Although there was a lamp in the shanty, there was no kerosene to fuel it and so the household had been retiring at dusk each day. The arrangements called for me and the mother to occupy the bed while the father, Abe, and his brother, Moses, were to sleep on the earthen floor. Charlie and Faga's youngest, a boy of two and a half years, had remained with his grandmother when the others left. The old woman stated that the boy would also occupy the bed. She declared that conditions at Charlie's place were so foul the child might not long survive there and she intended to keep the boy with her for the time being.

In the fading light I surveyed my dreary surroundings. How could these people, unwashed, with little to eat, dressed in tatters, coarse and illiterate, escape the doom which already held them by the throat? The holes in the walls and roof of the place were stuffed with bits of paper in hopes of keeping some of the flies out. How could they expect to last out the coming winter in this structure, I wondered. Dear friend, had there been revealed to me at that moment my involvement in the solution of this particular problem, I would have run screaming into the night.

The sleeping places prepared, everyone went outside to relieve himself. There was no outhouse or latrine. Each one simply picked a place in the prairie grass.

Returning, everyone went immediately to bed. I hoped to delay joining them but six people in a twelve-by-fourteen foot space leaves little room to walk about or even stand. Quickly, the darkness became total and I had no choice but to retire. The boards of the bed, without mattress or spring, were covered with straw which pricked my skin at the least movement but did little to ease the hardness of the bare boards. Still what bothered me the most was occupying the same bed with the old lady, a person whom I had never even known until a few hours ago. I lay as stiff and unmoving as I could while the sound of snoring rose to an ever higher crescendo until it seemed that the very walls shook.

Suddenly I began to feel quite warm. The little boy had emptied his bladder and quickly followed with a healthy bowel movement. I removed myself as far as possible from these immediate surroundings and gave myself up to utter despair. As the tears ran down my cheeks I reflected upon the course of my miserable life.

My early childhood passed through my mind, the time of the servant girl and then my cruel stepmother, followed by the seven years with my religiously fanatic grandfather. Within memory I could not recall having lived in a house which I could call home. Little tenderness had ever been shown me. I had tried so hard to raise myself to a decent life but my way seemed ever downward until now my existence was hardly above the level of an animal.

Dear God, I thought, whatever your reason, haven't I suffered enough in my nineteen years to pay for the rest of my life? The home I had always so desperately sought still eluded me. The people, the overwhelming prairie, America itself, seemed strange and terrible. I had no place to turn. There were no other homes to be seen on the vast expanse of the great plain. Except for one family, the only people who lived within miles were the Calofs. Where could I turn for friendship? Even my intended could not openly champion me. He was in his parents' home and tradition denied him an independent voice in the home of his parents. In just two brutal days the pioneer life had brought me to the brink of desperation. Yet as always, a spark of resistance to my lot and a core of determination remained within me, and by morning I was prepared to continue toward my goal. Despair gave birth to courage. Thank God. I would have great need of it before long. Time and again my resolve was to be tested to the limit.

Abraham and Charlie were the first of the family in America and had brought their parents and brother, Moses, to North Dakota only three months earlier. Even though Abraham had not actually seen his family for three years, they had been in touch and involved and were not strangers to one another. I was the only alien there and I realized that my welfare would in many ways be entirely my concern.

I began the following morning by protesting that I could not

29

again sleep with the child. The grandmother answered briefly and decisively. This was the way it must be, and the sleeping arrangement would continue. I understood then I was not to speak of this again, but I knew I was stronger for having expressed myself and would better face up to the tests which I knew were ahead.

The very next day brought a new blow. The men held a meeting to make plans for getting through the winter. They decided that Abraham was to work three months at the homestead of the one settler in the area who was not a Calof. His place was five miles or so distant. He was better off than most and had offered seventy-five dollars for three months' work on his homestead which was already under cultivation. This money could provide the necessities which would enable the three Calof families to survive the winter. I raised my voice against the arbitrary selection of Abraham. Why not one of the other two brothers, I demanded to know? The answer was swift and certain. Women, I was informed, had no judgment or voice in matters of importance. Unmistakably the subject was closed, but at least all concerned had learned that I had a voice and the will to use it where my welfare was concerned.

I accompanied Abraham to his place of work and after a few parting words began my return. That walk back across the lonely prairie proved to be a momentous testing for me. A veritable torrent of emotions flowed through my mind. Except for Abraham's return for a few hours on weekends, I would be alone in the terrible new world in which I now lived and I would have to fight my battle without my only ally. Looking across the great plain, I knew a loneliness which seared my very soul. Who belongs to me and to whom do I belong, I questioned? I was young and healthy and had always had a zest for life despite my meager past. Still these qualities seemed inadequate to lead me out of the nightmare existence into which I had fallen. I sat on a stone in the high grass and gave myself up to utter despair. So great was my anguish that sense of time and place faded from my consciousness. There remained only a void of misery and I prayed with a terrible intensity to God to show me mercy and the way to a better life.

After a time the storm of my emotions passed and I arose from the ground. My mind was clear and calm. The resentment and rebellion born in the last two days had solidified into a new strength which was to serve me well from that time forward. I had no illusions about the events which surely awaited me, but I knew now I would never surrender to the overwhelming conditions facing me. I would not become like the others. My desire for a better life would not desert me.

Upon my return, Abraham's mother noted my tear-stained face and admonished me that to cry for personal reasons was a sin before God. With my new *chutzpa* (nerve) I responded that her disapproval of me was of little importance. I told her that I had nothing further to lose and that her acceptance of me mattered little. Again she reprimanded me, this time for my unseemly speech, but I didn't care. I looked at the people there and I felt rebellion boiling within me. When my eyes lit on the little *pisher* (bed wetter), I knew strong and satisfying emotion. I felt I was his enemy.

As night approached I told the old lady that I was not content to go to bed at sundown. I informed her that I would try to bring light into the shack. I went outside to see what materials nature might provide for my project, and soon found some partly dried mud which I molded into a narrow container. I shaped a wick out of a scrap of rag, smeared it with butter, placed it in the mud cup, and lit it and, lo and behold, there was light. Everyone was delighted with my invention. Now we could retire at a more reasonable hour. Now we were able to undress and prepare for bed in a civilized way. This

31

accomplishment stands out in my mind as the first result of my effort to climb out of the mire which surrounded me.

Having now gained status in the household even though I was both young and only a woman, I sought to further improve the household conditions. Seeing that the old woman had not even a bit of candle with which to greet and bless the Sabbath, I made a number of my mud lamps which not only solved the ritual problem but also added to the light in the room.

I saw Abraham only on the weekends in the ensuing weeks. When he would leave to return to his work, my spirits would fall to a low ebb. One time, in the middle of a week which was proving to be a particularly difficult one, my resolve came to the fore again and I decided to visit my boyfriend at the farm where he worked. I only had a general idea of the way and there was no road to follow, but I set out regardless in the late afternoon.

I was thrilled at the idea that for once we could see one another and talk all by ourselves without the prying eyes and ears of the others. I walked through the tall prairie grass, through wild underbrush, over stony places, and through swampy areas as well. I was lucky to find the way. Finally I came to a cultivated field and saw someone in the distance. I cried out and ran forward. Yes, it was Abraham. We were overjoyed to see one another. Poor Abraham, he looked so weary, so worn out. Sweat poured from him. He had been shocking grain. His job was to pick up the bundles from the binder and put them into shocks. He was working with two binders, which was very hard work.[11]

After a few minutes, following our joy at seeing one another I sensed that he was becoming troubled and nervous. "Go back," he said, "before Anderson, the boss, sees you." Anderson was due on his rounds momentarily, Abraham said, and he would not put up with visiting on the job for which he was paying twenty-five dollars per month. Still, it was a very satisfying experience for both of us. Abraham said that he intended to start for home the following Saturday after the day's work was done, and I decided then and there that I would meet him on his way home.

Late Saturday afternoon I informed Abraham's mother that I was leaving to meet him. To my credit, she raised no objection. The afternoons were becoming chilly but unfortunately I had no warm clothing. I wasn't concerned however, as I felt that I knew the way and could easily detect Abraham coming from the opposite direction.

Something went wrong though and soon I become completely lost, and in the fading light I stumbled into a swampy area where the grass grew taller than my head. The swamp frogs began their night serenade and the cries of the birds overhead were lonely and mournful. My imagination began to play tricks on me and I began to believe that I heard the sounds of wild animals. I was thoroughly frightened and tried frantically to work my way out of the swamp, but whichever way I turned my feet seemed to sink deeper into the mud. The old country superstitions came to my mind that devils took advantage in these conditions to lead a lost traveler deeper into the swamp. Such thoughts could bring one to panic and I tried to put them from my mind. It had now grown totally dark. I wanted to call out but I was fearful of attracting wild animals. I continued to flounder in the dark, seemingly getting further into the swamp.

Realizing at last that I was badly in need of help, I began to call Abraham's name at the top of my voice. But all I heard in return was a faint sound which sounded to me like the echo of my own voice. I stumbled into a large rock on to which I climbed, meanwhile crying and praying to God and shouting Abraham's name in a continuous uproar while my despair

33

grew. Abraham did hear me though. I had actually come within earshot of his working place. The work had taken longer than usual and he was about to leave. No sooner had he walked out of his boss's house than he heard my voice, although he said my yells were so piercing that they seemed to come from all directions and he had a hard time determining where I was and how far away. In trying to follow my cries to their source, he himself began to lose his way. There were no landmarks or lights. To lose your way on the prairie was like being lost at sea.

I remained seated on the rock, cold, scared, and wet, but my voice if anything was growing in volume. Suddenly there was a movement immediately before me. In one final effort I screamed his name, but it was Abraham. He appeared as though he had descended from heaven. He said that he was about to turn in another direction when my last shriek finally led him to me. I think that I was very lucky that night. The few houses on the prairie were seven or more miles apart and I would not have been the first traveler in North Dakota to lose his way and possibly his life if Abraham had not rescued me. Nothing is done without our heavenly Father, who led Abraham to me through that wilderness.

Winter was very near now. Abraham had earned his seventy-five dollars. This was the money which hopefully would buy sufficient fuel and food to carry three families (nine people) through the winter. It looked like it might just be done. Prices were reasonable. Flour sold for ninety cents per one-hundred-pound sack.

The roof on our shack was now built and on the basis of this security Abraham and I set our wedding date for November 8, 1894. Our shack, however, was now in a different location because of a development which occurred earlier in the summer. During the warm months we had dug a well close to Abraham's parents' place. The well was about equidistant between the shack of Charlie and Faga and ours, about one-half mile, a long way to carry water. Soon after this well was dug it was discovered to be on land belonging to the state. We then dug another well five miles further into the free land territory and moved our shack there. Six weeks before we were married, Abe and I each filed claims in this new area.

The law provided that a homestead claim could be filed as late as five years from the time a homesteader settled on the land, but I had only the six weeks before my marriage in which to file my claim. Married women whose husbands owned or were claiming land were denied homestead claim rights but single women had the same rights as men. Abraham's land would be in his name but mine would be in my maiden name. Shortly after the new well was dug and our shack was relocated on the new land, Abraham and I started out for Devils Lake, the county seat, to file our claims.

This was a memorable trip for us and I remember it vividly to this day. We drove with the three oxen, which were mutually owned by the three families, hitched to a wagon which was used in the field. The wagon was equipped with wheels for warm weather and runners for the coming winter. For one reason or another, the wheels were not usable at that time and so the runners were attached instead. The prairie was cold and wet but there was no snow and the poor oxen had a hard, slow time pulling this contrivance across the grass and mud. The bottom of the wagon was spread with the usual straw for our traveling and sleeping comfort.

Night fell at about the halfway point of the journey. The oxen were weary and we could go no further until dawn. It was cold and wet, but at least the cattle were enjoying the stop, eating their fill of the rich prairie grass. Our hotel room was roomy. Its floor was the never-ending prairie and the ceiling was the vast vault of the sky. It was very cold and the dew fell like rain. We had only an old quilt and a smaller cloth to cover us, and only a little food to eat. We had taken no more than was thought essential since supplies were very scant at best and it was necessary to preserve as much as possible for the coming winter.

We were happy to greet the new day. Hitching up the oxen, we continued at a better pace and soon were in Devils Lake. We filed our claims without difficulty and we felt a sense of accomplishment. It was already about two o'clock in the afternoon and time to start our return trip across the grass desert. We were already exhausted though. We had had little food since we started and nothing hot to drink. When Abraham suggested that we go into a place for a cup of coffee, he didn't have to beg me very long, believe me. We still had a little bread left and I remember with pleasure sitting in that little place drinking coffee and eating our bread. It was a very nice experience.

That night again camped on the open prairie on our way back, I felt encouraged to confide in Abraham how the experiences of North Dakota had affected me. I told him that this trip to Devils Lake had heightened my resentment and discouragement at the prospect of returning to the depressing conditions which we had left just two days ago. Abraham sighed regretfully. He was very sympathetic and vowed that some day our lives would be better. I did not take much comfort in the phrase "some day," but I was pleased by his concern and sensitivity. I told him in return that he need not worry about me anymore, that I stood by his side and together we would attain a decent life. Of course I knew that the problems ahead were as deep as an ocean, but our talk under the stars fortified me and by the time we reached our destination I felt a pride of ownership in the land which we had claimed.

36 Our way was without end, beset with problems big and

small, and soon we were faced with one of serious proportions. Again it was found that Abraham and I had settled on state land.[12] We were permitted to finish the winter out in this location, but in the spring we would have to move to new claims which we were assured were a valid exchange for the land we were giving up.[13] We were notified that we would have to cover the well which we had so laboriously dug, and in the spring we knew we would endure the hell of beginning all over again. We had already done much work on these acres, but of course all of this labor would be lost to us. Despite this setback, our spirits were on the rise. We were striking out on our own. That was the important thing. So we believed, not knowing that our home regularly would be shared with others for many years to come. But now we labored from dawn to dusk preparing the new land which was to finally be our home. These days passed swiftly, though, for we believed we were at last creating our own future and we were inspired with a new stimulation and purpose. We were also excited about our approaching wedding day.

Finally the day came. The wedding, my friends, was a knockout. Since Abraham's niece, Doba, had the largest home with two rooms, she offered her palace for the occasion.

My soon to be in-laws, spreading their usual cheer and good will, insisted that the bride and groom had to fast until the ceremony was completed. I was instructed to say my prayers with tears and to implore my dead parents, or at least my departed mother, to attend my wedding.[14] This whole business brought me much distress and, even more, the realization of the family's influence over every aspect of my life, my wedding ceremony included.

My bridal gown, which I had made myself, was of yellow, blue, and white stripes. Abraham's suit hung so low in the back that it might have passed for what is today called "tails."

37

Those in attendance were Abraham's family, his nieces, Doba and Sarah, and their husbands and their two children. Also present were two families who were about ten miles distant from us. Our wedding gifts were a red felt tablecloth with green flowers, two chickens, and from Charlie and Faga two short women's undershirts. A delayed gift of some little chicks was also promised for next spring by one of the nieces.

The wedding feast was cooking in the kitchen and as the day was coming to a close the wedding was close at hand.[15] The Jewish man certified to perform the ceremony was a member of one of the Jewish families in North Dakota.[16] My fiancé had to work for him for two days hauling hay in payment of his fee.

All brides remember their wedding ceremony and mine was truly memorable. I was seated in a chair. Abraham was given a flour sack which he was instructed to place over my face.[17] Well, at least one could cry in private under the cover.

Being effectively blinded, I was now led to the *huppah* (the wedding canopy) by Doba and her husband. The *huppah* was built of a shawl tied to four sticks.[18] The music was provided by the singing of the women while the men beat time on tin pans.

Following the ceremony the table was set and we sat down to a truly magnificent banquet which consisted of beans, rice with raisins, chicken soup, and roast chicken. The flour sack had been replaced by a handkerchief bound over my eyes. I wanted to remove it to at least be present at my own marriage, but my mother-in-law was quick to forbid it. I did not want to create a scene at my own wedding and so I submitted to these primitive customs. Later, I was to learn that the women present considered me impudent to have made such a suggestion.

The festivities over, bride and groom started home, and in short order, even before my wedding day was over, I was cruelly thrust back into the reality of my life. I learned that the

Calof men had decided prior to my marriage that Abe and I must share our home with others for the entire coming winter. What horror. Had any bride every been more grossly betrayed on her wedding day? This decision resulted from the belief, I was told, that the fuel supply would not be adequate to heat all three shacks through the coming winter and, therefore, Abe's father, mother, and brother Moses would double up with us for the coming months.

In an instant the happiness of my marriage turned to bitterness. The knowledge that I was to spend my honeymoon in a tiny space shared with three strangers was more than I could bear. I hoped that death would take me now, that I would not reach home alive. But my fervent wish was not granted, and it was life, not death, with which I had to cope.

The furniture and arrangement in Abe's and my home was the usual. Two beds, one belonging to my father and mother-in-law and the other for Abe and me, were hammered to the walls. Between the beds stood a table also hammered to a wall. The remaining pieces of furniture were a short bench and the stove. The seating arrangement for meals called for one person on each of the beds while the other three would sit on the bench. Moses would sleep on the ground on a pile of straw.

We five people, however, were not to have such spacious quarters all to ourselves. At this time the in-laws had a flock of twelve chickens and Abe and I also had twelve. There was no outside coop for the poultry, but if there had been we would have lost the flock in short order because the tempera-ture would soon be going to forty or more degrees below zero and the chickens would have frozen to death. We needed to keep them alive in hopes of having their eggs as well as their meat later on. Each family was to keep its chickens under its bed and the ends and sides were closed off to form a cage. Also there was a calf which had to be accommodated inside.

39

It occupied the remaining corner opposite Moses's sleeping space.

This is how five human beings and twenty-five animals faced the beginning of the savage winter of the plains in a twelve-by-fourteen-foot shack. This is how we lived and suffered. The chickens were generous with their perfumes and we withstood this, but the stench of the calf tethered in the corner was well-nigh intolerable.

The fuel supply for the three families was one ton of soft coal which would be split between the two shacks. When this was exhausted we faced the prospect of simply freezing to death. For staples we would depend on the chickens, three one-hundred-pound sacks of flour, and one sack of barley. The main part of our diet was bread and anything else which could be made from flour.

A minimum of fuel was used during the waking hours but none at all at night, and in the mornings icicles hung everywhere, which melted and ran down the walls from the heat of the morning fire.

The winter was not far advanced before I found myself pregnant and so ill that I could hardly tolerate such a diet.

Words are useless to describe the nightmare of those months. I can only say that when March arrived we still lived.

At this time the men formulated a new plan. Our guests were to leave us and to begin with Charlie the repair of the shacks which had been damaged by the winter storms. However we were not permitted to be totally free. Faga, Charlie's wife, was sent to stay with us since she would be of no help in the repair work and would only be in the way.

As I continued into my pregnancy, my illness worsened. I developed a severe cough and began to spit up blood. I became very frightened at seeing this and Faga suggested that I build up my health by drinking milk. This should have posed no problem since each of the families owned one cow, all of which had lived through the winter. However when my in-laws left they took Abe's cow and left Charlie's cow with Faga. Even though she had encouraged me to drink milk and was supposed to share the milk with us, she showed such selfishness when the milk was divided that I did pretty much without, and I recovered from my illness, also without anyone's help.

My spirits rose with the promise of spring and the improvement in my health. I began casting about for something to do which would improve our lot. One of our big problems was our water supply. We had dug three wells, each to a depth of seventy-five feet with poor results. Now our water supply was so scant that I decided to find some usable water in some low place on the prairie where the snow melt might run together. I did discover such a place about a mile away. I carried two pailfuls from that place, but when I got back to the shack I saw that the water was full of worms and grass. The water would have to be boiled to be usable. The solution to the problem was not so easy as we had just run out of fuel. There was nothing with which to start a fire. I was determined though, and again went out into the prairie which held many provisions if one only knew where to look. I took with me only a rope and my huge belly.

About two miles distant I came across a place where new grass was growing through a bed of dried-out grass. The dried grass was plentiful and looked dry enough to burn. I was delighted with my find. My pleasure, though, was tempered with a certain dread. I knew little of the wildlife of this country, and I became fearful that I would encounter a snake in the beds of dried grass. I hesitated, but soon my stomach informed me how hungry I was, and the child within me needed food too. My husband labored in the field removing rocks and I knew that he too must be hungry. I needed that boiled water to

41

prepare some kind of a meal and I said to myself, "Don't be a spoiled person. You must risk it. Even if there is a snake there, you must try." I stepped into the area. No snake bit me and soon I was enthusiastically gathering the dried grass. Quickly I gathered a great bundle and tied it into a compact bundle with my rope.

According to the sun it was already midmorning and Abe would be coming in from the field not long after noon. I had to get home quickly but the food left in the shacks was only a little flour, some barley, some soured milk, and a little butter. A really daring idea came to me. I decided to spend a little more time looking around the place to see what else it might offer. Promptly, my further exploration brought results. I found what appeared to be wild garlic. I was delighted and ate a kernel. It tasted wonderful and didn't seem to harm me, so I gathered quite a number of bunches. My ambition by now was really on the rise. Bread and garlic alone make a poor meal. I enlarged my search area and before long I came across plants which unquestionably were wild mushrooms. Now I knew that some mushrooms were deadly poisonous. Still I thought that this was a good time to take a chance. I bit into one and held it in my mouth. It didn't burn or taste bad, so I swallowed it. I waited a while for something to happen. Nothing did, and I gathered an apronful of the mushrooms, and with my garlic and the bundle of dried grass on my shoulder, I started for home happy with my accomplishments and eager to see how I could put them to use.

Arriving at the shack, I immediately began my preparations. First I sieved the water through the fabric of a flour sack. I kneaded the dough and put it in the oven. I cleaned the mushrooms and steeped them in hot water. I then chopped up the garlic, put butter (we had our cow back) in the pan, and fried everything together. This meal made in large measure with food gathered from the wild prairie was simply delicious.

I should have mentioned that Abe had begun to dig a cellar in the dirt floor of the shack. It was as yet not completed and boards had been laid on the edges of the hole. When the project was completed we would at last have a wood floor with a cellar beneath.

I was so excited in preparing this special meal that I nearly fell into the pit as I flew about the place, setting the table and making other preparations. We had no tea or coffee, but I ground up some barley, boiled it in water and so had, at least, a substitute coffee.

My husband would soon be coming through the door. I was so happy, truly in seventh heaven, and very proud. I had used my brains and my nerve and as a result my husband would soon sit down to a fine dinner, just the two of us alone.

Soon Abe arrived. It was evident that we liked one another, because when he came inside where I was, it was easy to see that he was glad to see me and we were happy to be together.

Never was there a more delightful dinner than that one. The food was delectable and our shanty was filled with happiness. After we finished our meal, Abe insisted on knowing all the details of my accomplishment. As he listened, his gladness became tinged with a sadness that our condition was such that I was reduced to searching the prairie for food. But nothing could destroy the magic of that hour. He kissed me and called me his good angel, and my contentment was complete knowing that he appreciated my devotion to him. I served the barley coffee in the cool outdoors and we spent another pleasant hour together before Abe returned to the field. So ended a charming interlude in the harshness of our lives. It was a great moment for us and its memory has been a sustaining treasure to me over the years.

43

As the time for the birth of my child drew closer, I began to weigh the uncertainties which faced me. If there were to be any serious problems in the birth, either for the infant or myself, one or both of us could die since there would be no skilled help available to us. I knew that if difficulty arose, the people around me could offer little or nothing in the way of meaningful help. I didn't even have a suitable cloth in which to wrap the little child upon its arrival. I must say that each day my doubts and fears increased as my time moved ever nearer.

My mood became sad and doubtful and I began to suffer fits of bitter crying. But before long my disposition changed and I faced the coming event with a better attitude. I was determined to do the best I could to improve our living conditions before the arrival of the child. In the following weeks I continued to gather and store the dried grass. I hauled water a long ways for use not only for cooking, but to make the shack as clean as I could. I felt the effects of hauling these heavy loads but I persisted. At this time our main food was cheese which we made from the milk which soured in one day in the hot weather.

Abe's thoughts ran parallel to mine. We got along so well when we were left alone. Soon the cellar was finished and a wooden floor laid. This was a significant step in our struggle to improve our lives. I cried again, but this time with happiness.

Now I turned my attention to the walls and ceiling. The dirt which was removed in digging the cellar was mainly clay and I thought to use it to fill the cracks in the walls and to make them smoother. The clay would harden quickly in the hot weather, I reasoned, and with God's help we might then be able to get some whitewash with which to paint the walls. My ambition soared. I could already visualize how clean and pretty my home would be.

44

I told Abe of my plans. He was as enthusiastic as I but was

concerned that the work would be too hard for me in my condition. We both understood that he could not help me very much. He was working in the field from dawn to dark with his father and brother, Moses. I assured him that I was capable of doing the work.

Early the next morning I prepared a pile of clay and began to knead it with my feet. I had refined it to a suitable mixture by the time Abe returned from his work in the evening. Although he had labored all day, he helped me haul water to add to the clay and then he worked far into the night hammering slats to the walls. I worked the moistened clay onto the walls, between the slabs, making a smooth inner finish over the rough boards. Finishing, I surveyed the result. A miracle had taken place. Our rude shanty had become a palace. The walls were not white but I was confident they would become lighter as the clay dried.

Abe's family came to view my handiwork and they praised me generously. They could not take their eyes from my handsome walls and clean floor. My mother-in-law alternately smiled and sighed. I believed she felt her old age and knew that such an accomplishment was beyond her. Thus the second summer saw some improvements in our fortunes. We had brought in a small crop of hay and now had improved our home. Still, in general, our circumstances remained desperate.

Already the men were planning for the coming second winter [1895–96]. The prospects appeared even more grim than for the first winter. Again the two great concerns were food and fuel sufficient to carry us through the terrible months.

The men hitched the oxen to the wagon and made a tedious three-day trip to Devils Lake to sell the combined hay crop. They received a disappointingly low price for it with which they were only able to buy one-half ton of coal, one hundred pounds of flour, twenty-five pounds of sugar, some yeast, and a little coffee. Nine people would have to depend on these meager supplies, augmented by the always scant store of food on hand to live through to the spring.

Abe was offered fifty dollars for two months' work at a distant farm to help with the threshing and do other work. He assured me, though, that he would not leave me until the baby was born. He didn't want to forsake me at all, but circumstances ruled otherwise.

As my time drew near I asked Abe to invite his mother to attend me at the time of delivery. I, personally, was totally ignorant about the entire subject matter. It may be hard to believe, but I was soon to learn that she, a mother of four, knew as little about a confinement as did I.

Ten days later, at four o'clock on a Saturday morning, I brought forth my first child, Minnie. I had a hard time and literally tried to crawl up the walls with the pain of it. Abe assisted me as best he could and it was he who cut the umbilical cord. He was delighted that I had given him a daughter. As for myself, I was more preoccupied with the serious problems which I knew faced both the little girl and me.

By eleven o'clock, seven hours after the birth, the child and I were alone, left to our own resources. My mother-in-law had returned to her shack and my husband was back in the field. But what of the mother who had just borne her first child? There was no one to help us. I looked at my first born, unwashed as yet, wrapped in a scrap of my old skirt, and knew that I had to get back on my feet quickly. I arose and cleaned myself up as best I could. I prayed that my mother-in-law would soon return to help me care for the child. I felt deserted and frightened and was conscious of a terrible weight on my shoulders. I was overwhelmed suddenly by the dreadful prospects facing my little infant born into such a hostile world. My

Charadh Kalov, Rachel Bella Calof's
mother-in-law, at the age of 91.

mood of despondency was unhealthy and, as you will soon
know, was the onset of a fearful illness of the mind, a sickness
which was fed by the fanaticism and superstition to which I
now found myself subjected.

My mother-in-law was a religious fanatic and superstitious
beyond imagination, and the force of her dark beliefs and
suggestions found me terribly vulnerable in my already-dis-
tressed state of mind. When she left me alone that morning she
placed a prayer book in my bed. She explained that this was to
prevent devils from harming me and taking the baby. This
suggestion was the seed from which grew the central theme of
my coming ordeal.[19]

47

The old lady returned. She brought bread and milk but refused to warm the milk for the baby because it was the Sabbath and lighting a fire was considered a prohibited labor. My husband was not allowed to visit us and ate his meals that day with his brothers away from me. On these notes the Sabbath drew to a close.

When night fell I begged for a little heated water to wash the baby and again for warm milk to feed her. The warm water request was refused because there were no stars in the sky which, I guess, was a bad omen for the washing of babies.[20] However, the old woman after again checking the sky finally consented to warm some water. She chose to use an old rusted pan from which she attempted to remove the rust by scouring with ashes from the stove. I was afraid that the infant would get blood poisoning from this water but I washed her upper body anyway.

The mother-in-law now prepared food for us. She made *taiglach* (noodles) and milk and cooked a piece of chicken in the same rust-streaked pan in which she had just heated the water.[21] I was quite hungry and looked forward to having something with which to feed the baby as well. My anticipation was short-lived. The cooked chicken was streaked and besides smelled very strange. I wouldn't eat this food, and I certainly would not put any of the liquid from it in the child's mouth. Even the old woman admitted the food smelled rotten, but she attributed this to the belief that the chicken had probably not been killed in the prescribed kosher manner.

Unfed and dirty, the child and I lay on the straw bed which was covered with a sheet. As the night deepened and became colder, my mother-in-law refused us the luxury of a fire in order to save fuel and instead covered us with an old coat and a gunny sack.

48

The child remained quiet the next day. As yet I had not

heard her cry, and as the day progressed I became more and more alarmed that she was sick. I was afraid to really examine her but I finally got the nerve to unwrap her entirely. I became ill when I saw that her little body was stuck to the wrapper. When I saw her navel I screamed in terror. I thought that her intestines were falling out, but it proved to be the cord which was about twelve inches long. The old lady said that Abe had been afraid to cut the cord shorter for fear of harming the child. Overcoming my fear, I washed the child thoroughly and rewrapped her in a clean piece of the old skirt.

On Monday, two days after the birth, Abe left for his distant job. I was forlorn to see him go. The consequences of his absence were compounded by the fact that the wells had again gone dry. The closest water supply was five miles distant and the cattle would have to be led there once each day. We had a little well water left in the house for which I was really thankful because it was clean and contained no worms. For the first three days of her life, the only nourishment little Minnie received was sweetened water.

On the third day my milk came, but at the same time I became feverish and suffered considerable pain. My mother-in-law had me stoop over a heated stove to ease the pain. This was another of her old world cures and it didn't help at all. She departed soon to attend to her menfolks and again I was left to shift for myself. Before she went, though, she instructed me with great sincerity regarding the precautions which I must follow to protect the baby and myself from the contrivings of the devil. I must be certain to leave the prayer book in the bed with the child if I had to get out of bed. This was to prevent the devil from taking the child in my absence. For my personal protection from the fiend, I was to carry a knife at all times in a belt around my waist.[22]

You can imagine what fertile ground these whisperings

49

found in my mind already in disorder from the despondency which came to me following the birth. And so on the fourth day, when out of milk and with no food left in the house except flour and yeast, I went outside to milk the cow. The prayer book was in the bed and the knife was securely in my belt. The next day my mother-in-law gave me credit for my heroism. She seemed somewhat surprised that we were still present.

On Friday I baked bread knowing that my husband would be home on Saturday and stay until Sunday evening. I cleaned the house and milked the cow. Suddenly a great weakness came over me and I felt as though I was being drawn into the very depth of the earth. I crawled into bed with my little girl, both of us crying loudly.

That evening, after blessing the Sabbath candles at her place, my mother-in-law came to see how I was getting along. She was surprised to see my newly cleaned floor and freshly baked bread. She told me that I was a good person and offered me food but I was unable to eat. I felt so queer and frightened and the knife in my belt was a constant reminder of the devil's intentions for my child and me.

The old lady decided to return to spend the night with me after giving her men their supper. No sooner had she left than I seemed to develop a high fever. All the superstitious preaching of the last few days, as well as those of my own grandmother when I was just a tiny child, flooded my mind. My own fevered imagination added to the fantasies. I knew that there were demons who looked like little people and whose specialty was the stealing of newborn babies.

My hallucinations intensified and I became totally involved with the problems of guarding my baby from the demons who were intent on carrying her away.

When the old lady returned she prepared to sleep with me in the bed. She wanted to place the baby on the bench near the bed, with the prayer book of course. I refused to do this, carefully explaining to her that I would hold the child in my arms while wearing the knife in my belt, with the prayer book in the bed, all to provide the necessary defenses. She was as sincerely advising that the prayer book alone was sufficient for the protection of the baby. What a mad scenario. Two crazy people calmly discussing the best way to defeat the devil in his attempt to steal my baby. I was not convinced by her argument and held the baby tightly in my arms.

Shortly the grandmother was snoring deeply. The sound of it was frightening, particularly so when it began to sound less like snoring and more like devils whistling outside the cabin walls. My worst fears were realized. The demons had arrived. I must clasp the baby ever more closely to me, my knife at hand, prepared to defend my little daughter. So I remained, sleepless and on guard throughout the long night.

In the morning, the old lady refused to permit a fire to warm a little milk for me.[23] I drank the cold milk and prepared to care for Minnie. The child's grandmother left to care for her unfeeling men who had not even asked about us so far as I knew.

I returned to the bed and slept fitfully, the child in my tight embrace. The baby's crying awoke me. I felt an immediate thankfulness that she had not been stolen away while I was asleep.

I attended to the child and then warmed some milk for myself and ate some bread. Soon I had an urgent need to respond to nature's call. In the past days I had been able to attend to this matter while the old woman was with us. Now we were alone and the enormity of the problem almost overwhelmed me. I had to go outside into the deep grass. I was not prepared to accept that the prayer book would be sufficient protection to defend the child from the now ever-present demons. In the end I took the baby with me, laying her in the

51

grass close by. But now a new terror gripped me. The devil could easily have entered the house during our short absence. Would he snatch the baby as we came though the door? I had to steel myself for the ordeal of going back inside. I dashed in, slammed the door behind me, and leapt into bed with the child in a frantic continuous movement. I was badly shaken by the experience and felt sick and broken.

When the old woman returned later in the day she saw that I was quite sick, apparently with a high fever. She milked the cow for me,[24] after which she applied a wet cloth to my head. I'm afraid that the illness that had me in its grip required greater treatment than a cloth on my head.

As night drew near my apprehension became extreme. One final ray of hope remained to me, the presence of the baby's father. I awaited, frantically, his momentary arrival. He was my only friend and ally and my fevered mind told me that the child would be safe for the few hours he would be with us before he returned to his job for another week.

Soon, however, I was to be denied this last sanctuary for upon Abe's arrival his mother forbade him to see me. She insisted that he sleep that night in her house. I was considered still unclean so soon after the birth, and religious law prohibited him from sleeping in my bed or even approaching me.[25] Such was the fanatic's misuse of a simple rule of hygiene.

This was the final devastating blow which tore my mind from its last fragile hold on reality. From then on until the end of this terrible episode of my life, my only purpose for being was to win out over the devil for the possession of the child.

In justice to my husband, it is necessary to consider the kind of world we lived in, steeped in religious fanaticism, beliefs, and superstition. Our background was the harsh, unyielding culture of the poor and oppressed. In that world the rule of the parent was paramount, and a son—even a married man—did

52

not oppose his parents' wishes. Abe just could not go against his mother's decisions.

As Abe turned away, his mother remained long enough to warn me against revealing my mental anguish to him and said that if I did so he would have no recourse but to divorce me. Such was the religious law she told me.[26] What irony. More than any other cause it was her dark whisperings of devils and lost souls that had tumbled my mind into lunacy.

When Abe came by before returning to his job, I told him that I was not feeling well but I was careful not to disclose to him the torment which was consuming me.

My condition worsened daily. I lost weight rapidly and was unable to rest. I must be on guard every moment and ever more vigilant as Satan's friends became constantly bolder. Now they hammered against the door in the night and I saw them looking in the windows.

I lived in my world of madness for about six weeks. I found the physical strength to care for my child and myself and to tend to the household chores adequately, but my mind retreated ever further into the dark.

I worked constantly at improving my defense plans. As each day waned, I took my child in my arms and prayed frantically to God to shield us through the night. I then placed the baby in the bed and turned my attention to the physical protection of the house. The place had two small windows now, as well as a cellar, and a wooden floor. Entrance to the cellar was by means of a trapdoor built into the floor and a ladder. I hung rags over the windows to keep the demons from looking in. They already inhabited the cellar, at least at night, and I next gave careful attention to this point of entry into the house. I had searched for and found large stones weighing about one hundred and fifty pounds each and one of these I now rolled over the trap door. Another was set against the door. Finally I checked under the bed to be sure that somehow a demon had not crept in unbeknown to me while I was busy with my preparations. Following a final inspection I would fall into an exhausted sleep, only to be awakened by demons all around the house outside, pounding on the walls, whistling, and shrieking. "Give us your child," they screamed at me, "or else we will take you and the child." After a time the bedlam would subside and I would again sleep, only to be almost immediately awakened by even more insistent demands and louder shrieking and pounding. In this manner I spent night after night.

When Abe returned home again he saw the marked change in me. He was very concerned and insisted on knowing what was wrong with me. Remembering my mother-in-law's warning and with the cleverness of the deranged, I convinced him that my decline was due to loneliness for him. He tried to comfort me and reminded me that he would be home to stay in a few more weeks. Part of his mother's instructions to me regarding my state of "uncleanliness" was that I must be cold and distant to my husband and discourage any advances from him. Therefore, when Abe attempted to console me and attempted to kiss me, I pushed him away.

When the baby was five weeks old, Abe's job was finished and he returned home. He was a proud father. I had taken good care of the little girl and she was bright and healthy.

Abe's return brought relief in some ways to my mad concerns. Some problems also resulted. I no longer dragged the large stones into the house at day's end but instead piled the household goods and furniture on top of the trap door at night. Nor could I abstain from covering the windows. I countered all questions regarding these maneuvers with clever answers.

In this manner we continued about two weeks, until a Friday when there occurred an incident which, however terrible, probably set in motion events which led to my return to sanity.

Abe was in the field. There was much for him to do working and planning for the coming winter. I cleaned my house, baked bread, and then I nailed a newly acquired apple box to the wall to keep my dishes in.

Arranging my few dishes in the box, I stepped back a pace to examine the result and saw a little man dancing on the plates. What horror! In spite of my vigilance the demons were in my fortress. I seized the baby and ran howling from the house. So piercing were my cries that my husband heard them far across the field, and they reached to my mother-in-law's shack a long way off.

Abe was first to reach me. He held me close and gradually my hysteria subsided. But I was at the end of my rope. I could no longer bear my terrible burden alone. I was beyond such considerations as divorce and I poured out to him my dreadful fears and experiences. He was terribly shocked and did his best to reassure me. After a while he tried to lead me back into the house but I was terrified at what awaited me there. Abe tried to reason with me, but reason that day was far beyond my capability. How can I convince you, dear readers, that I saw the devil dancing on my dishes? In my eyes he was as real as anyone I have ever seen. Abe tried to lead me back to the house but I resisted.

Finally we reached an understanding. Abe would enter the house first and I would follow with the child. As I approached the doorway I felt that the baby and I were under a death sentence. Abe stayed at my side, constantly reassuring me, and after a while I recovered a semblance of calmness.

My anxieties did not leave me though, and it was arranged for one of Abe's nieces to spend a few days with me. Nothing could have been more beneficial for me, and it was her visit

55

which marked the beginning of my recovery. I owe so much to this fine woman.[27] Because of her I found the road back to the world of light. This wonderful person and I had been good friends from the moment we had met. She was always good to me. We seldom saw one another because of the difficulties of distance and the never-ending work which allowed little time for visiting, but when we were together she was always kind and generous. If she had a few pieces of sugar she shared them with me, and when she had a piece of white bread she shared that too.

She came on a Thursday and planned to stay until Sunday. I felt my heart lighten as soon as my friend came into sight.

As night approached I began to cover the windows. My dear guest asked in a gentle tone why I did this. No one covered the windows on the great plain where usually the closest neighbor was many miles distant. I confessed to her that I lived in mortal fear. When she asked me what I was afraid of, my reserve broke down and, through my tears, I told her the entire bitter story. She was struck with amazement at hearing of my experiences. "What are you saying," she cried. "You are a wonderful person. God is on your side. No harm will come to you. There are no devils," she assured me. Carefully and gently she questioned me, wanting to know how these ideas had become fixed in my mind. I replied that her own grandmother had warned me of the danger and that I had seen the evil spirits with my own eyes.

She arose and tore the rags from the windows, assuring me at the same time that such precautions were from this moment no longer necessary. I was appalled and was seized with uncontrollable fright. I pleaded with her to allow me to replace the coverings but she stood unyielding before the window and would not accommodate me.

Abe had built a cot especially for our guest. Despite the

panic I felt at the sight of the bare windows, her friendly matter-of-fact presence reassured me. She had brought candles with her, and at sundown the next evening we stood side by side and together blessed the coming of the Sabbath. The house was suddenly happy and bright, although I could not keep my eyes from those naked windows, still expecting to see the demons looking in.

My sweet friend, noticing this of course, said nothing for some time. She was thinking what she could do to reduce my fears. After a bit she asked if there were any *kissicks* (dried cow manure used for fuel) outside and, if so, I should bring some in since it might rain this night. I had not been outside in the evening for five weeks now and I replied that I was afraid to leave the safety of the house. Abraham would be coming in shortly, I told her, and he would bring in the fuel. Even as I refused her request, I realized she was trying to prove to me that my fears were groundless and my thankfulness for my friend grew.

Supper finished, she took my hand and said, "Come, let us go outside for a bit before we retire." I again drew back but she persisted. Holding my hand tightly she led me out of the house. I was stiff with fear but she spoke to me softly saying, "See there is no one here." I was only partly convinced and slept little that night, sensing that on the following day I would be further required to test the worth of my anxieties. However by the evening of the following day her quiet assurances and sympathy had so restored my confidence that I was now eager to again venture outside with my champion at my side.

When my wonderful friend departed on Sunday, she left behind a woman restored, cleansed of madness, ready to again face the rigors of the pioneer life.

Now for a short interlude, between past problems resolved and future difficulties soon to arrive, Abe and I lived in contentment, happy with our baby. Our euphoria was all too soon ended.

The first frosty signals of winter were already on the land and the men began their deliberations on how best to survive the coming months. In some respects, our resources were less adequate than those of last year. For one thing we had less than one ton of coal between three households.

I suppose, then, it came as no great surprise to me that Abe's father, mother, and brother Moses would again move in with us for the winter, but my torment was no less.

With the addition of Minnie to the winter group, the problem of living, and particularly sleeping, room would be even more stern than last year. Since more space is needed for sleeping than for sitting or standing, we decided to move the table and two benches outside each night. The baby's sleeping place was my special problem and I solved it by fashioning a hammock from a flour sack which I suspended from the ceiling over our bed.

The ordeal of this second winter, although similar in character to the first in physical suffering, introduced a new hazard to our lives, that of great tension. It was a more severe season than the previous one, extremely cold, with one howling blizzard after another, and it lasted almost six months. Moving around was impossible without rubbing and bumping against each other. Sanitation, bad to start with, deteriorated steadily as did our composure, and as the bitter winter wore on, our physical and mental states worsened.

Charlie's wife Faga, a *kvetch* (an ineffective person or whiner) at best, soon stopped baking bread in her shack on the pretense that their fuel supplies were too low to permit a fire hot enough for baking. Of course I was in a similar predicament, but I augmented my baking fire with straw which made for a hotter flame. I baked every day except the Sabbath, providing the bread for my household and Faga's as well. The cold was so intense that we made all the loose rags we had into mittens which we wore day and night.

The stove was fired up only while baking, during which time my mother-in-law would hang the men's frozen overalls near the stove to thaw them. As the ice in them melted and they began to warm, the foul smell added to our already unbearable atmosphere.

I put forth my best efforts to maintain some level of clean-liness in this hellish environment, but as you can well imagine, it was a battle doomed to failure. In retrospect I can understand the strain that Abe was under in the multiple roles he played in the small society of that shack. He was father, husband, son, and brother to us and he was the target of everyone's com-plaints and suggestions. It was an intolerable load and he finally sought relief by striking out at probably the only one there who was capable of receiving criticism. One day, like a bolt from the blue, he announced that he would have to divorce me because of the dirty condition of my house. Of course I know now that his action was a result of the stress under which we all lived, but when it happened I was in no mood to spend any time in analyzing the underlying reasons for his accusation. I was outraged at his charge and defended myself vigorously. I couldn't understand why he refused to recognize the impossible conditions which confronted me, and I stood face to face with him and gave as good as I received. I remembered his words with bitterness and tears for a long time to come. I had suffered many privations in my determina-tion to stand shoulder-to-shoulder with him, from Russia to this miserable shack, conducting myself under the most severe conditions as a Jewish woman should, and now to be threat-ened by divorce on the grounds of being dirty was to me the greatest degradation. Many events have faded from memory, but this insult remained.

But life and time do not stand still, and finally even this winter and its horror came to an end.

Late spring [1896] found my relatives back in their own place. I was immeasurably grateful to be mistress of my home again, however humble. I cleaned the place thoroughly, and then cleaned it again. I whitewashed the walls and made fine curtains for the windows from flour sacks. Abe somehow obtained some sugar, a real luxury, and everything began to look pretty good to me again. I guess you could say that I had an optimistic nature. Even though we had little left to eat, that didn't really matter much. What was really important was that we were alone again and managers of our own lives.

This summer was a good one in the development of the homestead. Through hard work and good trading, we acquired two horses. Yet, in the main, our condition was as delicate as before. We had little food or fuel and, of course, no money. We remained vulnerable to the harsh conditions which besieged us.

By August I knew that I was pregnant again but these were the stimulating days of summer and we were young and exultant in our youth. Our spirits soared and we visualized a more promising future than our past.

Hazard, though, was always close in those early days. Without warning, little Minnie was suddenly stricken with a violent illness. She threw up repeatedly and quickly developed an alarmingly high fever. Immediately we were faced with a crisis of decision. Should we risk a run to town with the child for medical help? The little girl's condition quickly became so serious that we were afraid she might not survive the rough trip. To summon and bring the doctor would take two or three days, and in any event his fee to come to our area would be seventy-five dollars, figured at one dollar per mile for the sixty-mile round-trip plus fifteen dollars for treatment. Such a sum was beyond our means, even if the doctor reached us quickly.

I frantically searched my mind for ways to help the child, but when I had exhausted my pitifully small store of medical lore the little girl's condition continued to worsen, and we feared for her life.

My means exhausted, I sat looking at my wonderful baby, my firstborn, with my thoughts flying wild in every direction. Incapable of hindering decline toward what appeared to be the baby's death, and unable to cope with such a reality, my mind chose to deal with the actualities which would follow. Where would I find a white sheet in which to wrap her little body?[28] And how would she be buried? I recalled the many stories I had been told of how the prairie wolves (people who knew called them "the butchers") on the day following burial on the open plain would pull the body from the grave and feed on the flesh and bones. If you think such thoughts were mad, you are wrong. They rather reflected the reality of life on the lonely plain.

Great was my anguish for my afflicted child, but God had pity and following a critical point in the illness the little one began to slowly improve.

For a short time during the remaining warm weather we lived in happiness and thankfulness for the continuing gift of our daughter.

Once again, at the threshold of winter, the decision was the same as before; the in-laws were to join us for another awful season. This time the overcrowding promised to be even more monstrous than in the previous winters. Minnie, now fully recovered, was a sturdy, active child. Last year she was an infant and spent the winter mostly in her hammock suspended from the ceiling. But now she was full of energy, needing space in which to move around. This was a serious problem but

61

obviously there was no solution for it. Even in her infancy, we could not shield her from the hard facts of pioneer life.

Before the winter began, though, my mother-in-law became ill with severe rheumatism and she also developed a bad cough. Her sons decided to take her to Devils Lake for medical attention and to arrange for her to spend the winter there.

Although Abe's mother had been little help to me in my first confinement, I knew I would miss not having an older woman at hand when the time came for the birth of my second child.

We evolved an arrangement for the coming event. It wasn't very complicated. After the birth, which was assumed to be solely my personal business, Faga would hold the umbilical cord while Abe cut it. The plan did not extend beyond this point.

I believe that the inadequacy of the planning became more apparent daily to Abe. As my time neared his doubts grew and he became increasingly nervous, until one day he abruptly announced that he would go to Devils Lake and bring his mother back to take charge.

It was now March [1898], a particularly cruel and treacherous winter month on the plains, liable to sudden and violent blizzards. The snow was very high and it was extremely cold. He intended to leave the following morning with our two horses pulling the field wagon.

I was very apprehensive about the whole affair. For one thing, I could have the baby any time now and the expectation of giving birth all alone in that great wasteland was a frightful prospect. Of equal concern was Abe's safety. Many people lost their lives in those terrible blizzards, wandering blinded and lost until they froze to death. I pleaded with Abe to abandon the scheme but he was determined to go.

The dependability of the two horses was also questionable. One, Topsie, was deaf and because of it very nervous. When

approaching him it was advisable to yell loudly and continu-
ously so as not to surprise him. At best he was always skittish,
and at worst hardly manageable. When he suspected that
someone was near he would pound the ground with his hind
legs until he heard the sound of a voice. The other horse was a
wild, unbroken bronco, high-strung and unstable.

Even emergency can provide opportunity. In our circumstances no opportunity was overlooked, and so the wagon was
loaded with some of the remaining stored hay. This cargo was
expected to bring one dollar and fifty cents. In turn, this
money would buy two gallons of kerosene, a bag of sugar, a
pound of coffee, and a supply of matches, all of which would
be divided between the three households.

You may wonder why one or even both of Abe's brothers did
not go in place of my husband, thereby permitting him to
remain with me so I would not run the danger of being alone
when the baby came. Much as I wanted to keep my husband by
my side, I realized that of the three only Abe had the courage
and determination to carry it off. The youngest brother was too
young and untested to undertake such a dangerous trip.
Neither was the eldest brother qualified since he lacked the
sense of purpose necessary to meet such a challenge. He would
have delayed leaving, and having gone might have turned
back.

The way to Devils Lake, across thirty miles of flat, open
prairie, totally lacking in guiding landmarks, was a challenge
even in fair weather. To attempt it during a raging blizzard was
to gamble with life itself. It was on such a morning that Abe set
forth. Within a minute he was lost from sight in the blowing
snow. As night fell, the intensity of the storm increased and the
snow flew so thickly that I could hardly see objects a foot or
two outside my window. In the following days, I prayed
fervently to God for my husband's safe return.

63

On the evening of the fourth day my prayers were answered. As I saw the wagon approaching, my joy was boundless and I ran to meet him. God meant for him to stay alive. His mother was with him and I wish to say that however much she and I differed in our philosophies of life, she earned my admiration for her fortitude in making the trip, particularly in view of her poor health. I thanked God for her safe arrival as well as Abe's. The old lady was so weak she could hardly stand and she was driven to Charlie's place to rest. Because of her condition it was decided that she would not attend me until the birth.

Two and a half days later, in the early morning hours of Thursday, I climbed onto my straw-covered "delivery" table to give birth to my daughter Hannah. The straw was prickly and cold, and as I labored I became thoroughly chilled. Abe had by now summoned my mother-in-law nurse. Seeing how cold I was, she ordered that a lid from the hot stove be placed close to me to warm me.

The first experience my poor baby knew upon entering this world was one of agony. Leaving her peaceful home in the womb, she was immediately plunged into intense pain and suffering. As she emerged, her elbow came in contact with the hot stove lid and she was severely burned. She was left lying on the table until the afterbirth came about a half hour later. My mother-in-law had a particular concern that the placenta would remain too long in my body, and her attention was directed entirely to this matter rather than to the baby. I recall straining and blowing into a bottle to hasten the process.

I believe now that during this entire time the infant was in contact with the hot stove lid. By the time we realized that the little one was injured, great damage had been done. The poor baby screamed until she had no voice left, only a sound like a mewing kitten. The child was wrapped in a cloth and placed near me, but I insisted on examining her to learn the cause of her pain and found a large hole burned into her elbow, with the burnt tissue already falling away from the area. The baby suffered terribly and she became dwarfed and shrunken by the hour.

This dreadful happening was only the forerunner of a combination of circumstances which in short order was to bring us all to the verge of total disaster. Although the winter was drawing to a close, it had been especially long and severe and now we were down to the last of our food and fuel. All in all, we were in a desperate way. Added to Hannah's injury and my own debilitated condition, we were now faced with starvation and freezing.

This was no time to be lying in bed, and the morning of the day following Hannah's birth found me on my feet prepared to deal with our difficulties as best I could. At the same time, Abe made ready again to leave for town with another load of hay to be exchanged for wood and food, and hopefully some kind of medicine for little Hannah. Having only one wagon, he could haul only a pitifully small load, especially of such a low-price crop. Even though the three families mutually owned two oxen and we had two horses, we still owned only one wagon between us.

Abe left before dawn hoping to complete the round-trip in two days, but as he reached town the dying winter spent its last energy in a great blizzard and he was forced to remain in town for almost two days. He had no money at all and was forced to take refuge in a barn. He did not return for four days, by which time we were literally starving and freezing.

When I got out of bed the day after the baby's birth, my first efforts were directed to gathering fuel with which to build a fire. I tried to gather the straw lying loose on the floor, but to my surprise I found myself too feeble even for this simple chore. I was much weaker than I was after the birth of my first child.

Leaning on the table for support, I surveyed our gloomy position and had to force down a rising tide of panic. The temperature in the shanty must have been close to freezing. My mother-in-law lay exhausted from the arduous trip through the blizzard. Little Minnie was pale and quiet. She had not eaten at all the previous day. Dominating the nature of the scene was the stench of rotting flesh from the infant's wound. All in all, we were in a desperate way.

I was finally able to start a fire with the straw still lying on the delivery table and now I turned my attention to the preparation of some food.

We had a cow by now but she was about to calve and gave no milk. You may question why we did not slaughter the cow or one of the oxen for food. I don't believe it ever occurred to anyone to kill and eat an animal that had not been ritually slaughtered according to the precepts of our religion.[29]

In the cabin were four sacks of grain seed, two of wheat and two of barley. These were to be used in the spring planting. They were to become our first food crops.

I ground up some of the wheat seed in the coffee grinder, running it through a number of times. It didn't much resemble wheat. It looked rather like a thick bran. I had to rest a while now before going on. I was weak to the point of collapse and my head and insides hurt terribly, but the hunger of my children and guest, as well as my own, drove me on.

I kneaded the dough and baked it in the oven, feeding the fire with my diminishing store of straw. I roasted some barley seed in the oven hoping to make a hot drink with it. I melted snow for this purpose rather than using the well water which was highly alkaline with a bitter taste.

My heart broke each time I looked at my little child,

Hannah. As yet she had had no food, and when the bread was ready I turned to her first. I broke a bit of the substitute bread into small pieces, poured black so-called coffee over them, and fed this mush to her. Such was the first meal for the newborn infant. She had not closed her eyes since her birth. The terrible pain she was enduring would not let her sleep.

At last Abraham arrived. He brought two buckets of coal, twenty-five cents worth of sugar, a pound of coffee, and some supposedly pickled herring which upon examination turned out to be, horror of horrors, pickled pigs' feet.[30] Considering our condition, you may draw your own conclusions as to whether Abe or I disclosed the true contents of the container which held this particular food. Also included in the bonanza were a pound of butter and, best of all, some ointment for Hannah's arm.

We were jubilant at our good fortune which seemed even greater considering its timely arrival. Indeed we cried with joy. Such was the nature of our stark and simple life. Little things made the difference between tragedy and happiness in a matter of minutes. Our lives were uncomplicated. Our purpose was survival, and through survival the hope that somehow the future would treat us more kindly than had our past. I did not inquire of my children born into that kind of world whether they considered their lives good or bad. My function was to raise them to a point in time when they could take charge of their own destiny. My role was basic motherhood. There was no time or resources for anything more.

As was our custom, we shared the food and even the few pounds of coal three ways.

I cannot say how much the medicine helped but miraculously Hannah's arm began slowly to heal. The mortified flesh continued to fall away for some time, but new tissue formed underneath and she improved.

67

I think that the children of pioneers came into the world with a certain hardiness of nature in preparation for the harsh conditions awaiting them.

As the weather moderated, Abe took additional loads of hay to town and we improved our food supply. Less fuel was needed as the days became warmer. He realized how close we had come to catastrophe and he was determined not to let it happen again if he could help it. He even insisted that his older brother Charlie carry a load into town. Abe tried hard to make the other men understand that he could not carry such a large measure of responsibility in providing for the three families. He warned the others that they must begin to contribute more to their own welfare.

The result of this was that Charlie did carry a load of hay to market, but he shared his purchases only with his parents and younger brother. I was not surprised.

The wilderness is always unpredictable, often unpleasantly so. The coming of spring weather found the prairie still covered by a great depth of snow. The rains came heavily one night and, with added snow melt, in a few hours the water was as deep inside the house as it was outside. I put both children on my lap, covered them with our usual stock of rags, and waited for the waters to subside. An umbrella would have been nice, but we did our best without.

Developments during the following summer again gave us added reason to hope that our chances of surviving on the land were improved. Abraham's share of the farmed land now was ten acres, a large part of which he had planted in wheat, and we estimated that our yield would be about two hundred bushels. We built a barn this summer and we had quite a lot of potatoes, which was my personal project, working in the potato patch with my children by my side. The cow had calved. Now we were getting milk and butter and these were especially welcome. Our new chicken flock rose to about fifty. This was our best summer by far. Considering that the weather was as extremely hot as the winter had been cold and that there were many hailstorms, we did very well.

In the fall the inevitable planning began for the following winter. The winters dominated our lives. It seemed that all our accomplishments during the warm seasons had to be directed to lasting through this one season. Even though this summer justified optimism in our view of the future, we were still in a weak position for the coming ordeal of winter.

Wheat was selling for thirty cents per bushel in town, but we had to retain some for our own use and, in addition, a certain amount had to be saved for seed.

I was able to send some of the eggs and all the butter to town for sale but butter was selling for seven cents per pound and eggs for seven cents per dozen. Although the sale of these dairy products would add to our financial position, you know that the produce from one cow at these prices didn't bring in much money. I would like to have preserved two or three pounds of butter for our later use but I had no way of keeping it fresh.

As the weather became colder, the chickens stopped laying and the cow gave less milk. The shadow of the coming experience was already spreading its pall over all of us, humans and animals alike.

Abraham now took most of our best wheat to market. The planning was to buy mainly coal and wood with this wheat money. Less needed to be spent for food, we reasoned, because we were now growing some of the staples which we had formerly had to buy. Abe returned with a good load of wood and some coal as well. The wood was green, though, and would require some drying. Close by our homestead was an Indian reservation.[31] There were trees on their land and the

69

Indians now brought us some green wood also. Probably they decided that we were going to persevere and now considered us as neighbors. I began a program of dividing my oven space between cooking and drying wood.

About now we had a bad setback. We had noticed that some of our wheat was growing poorly. As the summer season progressed this wheat began to actually grow smaller. Examination revealed that the roots seemed to be torn in two. We couldn't understand the reason for this. Finally Abe took the last of this remaining crop to town and there he learned that the wheat was no good. He was told that apparently the gophers were feeding on the roots and the wheat was unfit for seed. It was to prove unsuitable for baking as well, and we were left with only some oats for baking.

Well, as you probably have guessed, the talk once again was about the two families spending the winter together in our home. It made no difference that I was again pregnant. My in-laws were soon in their familiar winter quarters. Just imagine how hard it was for my two little girls. The baby, Hannah, was already beginning to walk and Minnie was an active, busy child.

This winter was also particularly vicious and long-lasting, and before it passed, despite our greater supplies, we had used all the wood and were again burning straw toward the end.

This pregnancy was a hard one for me. I was unable to rest or eat adequately all winter with seven people in a small room. Each time the crowding and dirt brought me to the brink of desperation, I focused my thoughts on the coming spring when I would again be queen of my castle.

I felt sure that my coming child was going to be a boy. So strong was the feeling that I began to make ready for the anticipated *bris* (the ceremony of circumcision). I prepared a garment for him for this singular ceremony and also a few diapers in honor of his coming. I also intended to make dresses for the two girls to wear at their brother's *bris.*

As soon as I was again the mistress of my own home I did my usual double spring housecleaning. After I had whitewashed the walls, I planned out my tailoring project. Shirts for the girls were cut from a flour sack and I fashioned dresses for them from an old black dress and from Abe's fancy shirt which he had worn in New York. It was in green and white stripes and added a gay tone to the dresses. Now the girls would be properly dressed for the ceremony.

My expectation proved right, and I gave birth to my first son, Mac, may he live and be well. Bringing a son into the world proved to be an expensive affair. The cost for the *mohel* (a religious technician who circumcises a male child eight days after birth) alone came to ten dollars, of which half was for his train fare to Devils Lake. The other five dollars represented his fee.

We had no money at all, but we were granted credit for the fee which was to be paid at a future, unspecified date. The train fare, however, would have to be paid immediately. After some difficulty, Abe was able to borrow this amount.

We now turned our attention to planning the festivities following this wonderful ceremony of the Covenant.[32] Of the most important consideration was the menu for the celebration dinner. It began on a moderate note. We had some cheese and butter and decided to roast two of our chickens as well. Compared to our usual fare, this was a real banquet.

But now suddenly a wonderful and spontaneous excitement seized us all, old and young alike. For years there had been little cause for celebration for any of us, and now it was as though a great yearning to be joyous, to reaffirm that life was worthwhile, was expressed through this festival. All the families joined in the planning and with the growing excitement came a certain recklessness.

71

It was decided that one of the jointly owned oxen should be slaughtered for the celebration. During the three years we had all been in North Dakota, none of us had tasted meat and everyone agreed that this would be a fine time to butcher an ox.

The forequarters would be shared by the three families and the hindquarters, considered not kosher,[33] would sell for three cents per pound in town. It was agreed that this money was to cover the cost of the event.

What a happy time this was. Abe left to bring back not only the *mohel*, but the *shochet* (the authorized slaughterer of animals according to kosher requirements) as well. We awaited the coming of these two functionaries with impatience.

The morning after their arrival, the *shochet* proceeded to slaughter the ox. Imagine our intense disappointment to learn that the animal was found to be *traif* (not kosher).[34] It was a terrible blow and in some measure affected the spirit of the occasion.

I had not fully recovered from the rigors of the birth, and after the excitement of the day was over I suddenly felt sick and weak. The *shochet* had been observing me closely, and now he approached and in strong terms ordered me to cook and eat the meat of the ox even though he, himself, had declared it to be *traif*. I was simply astounded. I could not believe my ears, but he carefully explained that according to his interpretation of the Jewish law I was obligated to eat the meat because I was sick and needed the nourishment not only for my own sake, but as a mother of small children I was morally bound to keep myself as healthy as possible so that I could better discharge my maternal duties.[35]

The *shochet* instructed me to salt the meat well before cooking it.[36] To tell you the truth I was absolutely delighted to hear his decision, but my joy was not shared by all. Even though only I was given the right to eat the meat, it was owned by all the families and each of the other two families was invited to take its share. My mother-in-law threw up her hands in despair and refused her portion. She believed that the *shochet* had taken leave of his senses. Her beliefs were so rigid she could not afford to compromise. Charlie, my brother-in-law, was not one to question my advantage and gladly took his share, but for the first time, at least in my memory, his wife, Faga, showed some spirit and informed him that she would not allow the meat in her shack. He had to assure her that he would cook the meat for himself away from the house.

My mother-in-law became increasingly agitated. She insisted that the *shochet* had betrayed his office. As for me, she promised that she would not even drink water in my house which would now be considered polluted. What a wonderful bonus. Everything worked out for the best, I thought. I had a delicious thought that maybe now she would refuse to move in with us next winter, and this proved to be the case. It would be an understatement to say that I was pleased.

I must say that personally the most dependable state of affairs I knew during the many years I lived on the prairie was pregnancy, and soon I was again carrying my usual load. I was determined that this pregnancy and birth would be better than the preceding ones. I was determined to carry on cheerfully with my work, but such was not to be. As my pregnancy progressed, the weather turned rainy and gray and I became vaguely fearful and despondent. As my time approached my depression grew. I prepared my delivery table as usual, spread with straw, but this time with a clean cloth on top, while at the same time crying uncontrollably. I felt certain that this time I would not come out of it alive.

I went outside to milk the cow and my tears mingled with the falling rain. I was overcome with a sense of hopelessness

73

and was unable to finish the milking or even strain the milk in the pail. I sent my father-in-law, who was nearby, for my husband, and then I held my three little ones close to me and prayed fervently to God to let me live for the sake of my children.

This time Abe, rather than his mother, attended me during both the birth and for the next several days. My new son was named Isaac, but in later years was called Jack. It should be noted, also, that Mac was named Moses.

The *mohel* was again summoned, but Abe did not leave my side. This time I was unable to leave the bed the day after giving birth as in the past. It was four days before I could get back on my feet. During that time Abe cared for the children and me.

Now, suddenly, Mac fell ill. He became feverish and developed a persistent rash around his mouth. He did not respond to what little medical care I had to offer. I didn't know what ailed him but I suspected that our diet, which was terribly limited, might be the cause.

My good friend, the *shochet*, was summoned. He was a clever man, more modern than most, and I had reason to know him as a good and humane man. He was only a slaughterer of animals but I had more faith in his medical advice than I could have in the drunken and brutal failures who practiced medicine on the frontiers.

The *shochet* first examined me and ordered me back to bed as I was still weak and ill. He decided that Mac's fever and rash were the result of having eaten something poisonous.

The following weeks were very hard. Mac became so ill he couldn't even swallow water. He lay in his crib and cried constantly. The new baby, too, cried a great deal.

My own physical and emotional strength returned slowly, but there was so much to do that necessity became the father of invention. Abe made a rocking chair mounted on runners so that I could work sitting down, meanwhile rocking the new baby and Mac. My hands were occupied with housework while my feet constantly rocked the children in my arms. I rocked without letup, even when I washed clothes. The girls too were dispirited and forlorn, and when my chores were finished I put them also on my lap and rocked and rocked while all the children cried and I with them.

They say that time cures all, and after a passage of many weeks my little family and I were whole again.

Despite our increasing hardships and setbacks, we were making slow but steady progress in establishing ourselves on the land. In the past we had farmed communally, but now each family had its own crops. Although we all joined in the common work of stacking hay, shocking grain, and engaging in other mutual tasks, we no longer shared the common wealth. The results of our labors belonged only to us.

Abe was a good manager. He had more grain to sell than the others. I tended the stock when he went to town, a trip which now took only two days if weather conditions were favorable.

Many days we worked side by side in the field with the little ones close by. Too, we had acquired more land and planned to have even more.

We now began actively to plan an adequate home and a carpenter was brought out from town to instruct Abe how to proceed on his own. As yet, we had so little money that we could not afford to hire the carpenter for the actual work.

Eventually, Abe, without prior experience, built a fine home for us with a full attic which became the children's bedroom and a full cellar as well. But this came to pass at a later date.

We were moving in the right direction but we had learned well the lessons of the past. We knew that sudden and fearful misfortune was ever close on the open prairie. We were terribly vulnerable and we never forgot it. Before this year had passed we would have another vivid reminder of our frailty.

This year [1900] we had planted most of the land in wheat. We had great expectations that this would be our first real crop. We dreamed that we would be able to build the dream house and even have enough money left for a few luxuries.

The wheat grew well and, at last, was ready for cutting. On a fine clear morning Abe checked our boundary lines[37] and made other preparations, for on the following morning we were to begin to reap the golden harvest. Our spirits soared. A better life awaited just ahead.

Dear reader, it was not to be. Before this day born in hope and promise was over, we had been sent reeling back into our former desperate state.

Shortly after the noon meal a dark cloud suddenly boiled up in the northwest sky. We both knew what such a formation could mean and we watched in fear and trembling as the sky became darker and assumed an ominous hue. Then suddenly the hailstorm, the scourge of the prairie farmer, was upon us. It was of such intensity that in a few minutes practically all for which we had suffered and labored so long was destroyed.

The wheat crop was hammered into the ground. The storm water washed away the grain which had already been cut and lay on the ground tied in bundles. Our two horses were killed running frantically into the wire which surrounded their pasture. The windows of the shack were smashed. Destruction was everywhere. We all, children and parents, huddled under the table for protection, but the shack became so filled with water we feared we would be carried away.

The storm passed as quickly as it came, and we surveyed the wreckage it had left behind. Ruin and desolation lay all about us. No wheat crop, no hay, the horses dead, the shack full of water, the windows broken out. The soil itself was torn and warped.

I suppose this was as good a time and reason as any to give up the long unequal struggle. But we had become resilient and tempered by hardships and, surprisingly, our first emotions were joy and thankfulness that we had been spared. We knew now that we could win out. We had come very close to success this time. Next year might well be the year of fulfillment. I looked at my children and was happy that we were still all in one piece.

A number of the settlers were unable to recover from this disaster and had to leave their land. Many cows in our area died of starvation that year as a result of the devastation caused by this storm, and many people suffered from hunger as well.

The lumber for our new home had already been delivered, and now we were unable to even begin to pay for it until some time in the future. But there it lay, and Abe decided to go ahead and start building as I was again expecting a child.

The calamity left us with little food except for our potato crop of which we had about one hundred bushels. We hoped that we would be able to buy seed for next year through the sale of some of these potatoes. Abe hitched the remaining ox to the wagon and hauled a load to town, but he was offered only five cents per bushel, and even at this price the buyer didn't want them. It seems that there was a glut of potatoes on the market because many farmers in the area who had lost everything in the great storm were trying to recoup, as we were, by selling off their potatoes.

Abe had no choice but to bring the load back, and potatoes became the main diet for both the cattle and ourselves during the coming winter. We had to obtain the seed by other means.

Abe worked hard to complete as much of the new house as possible before winter weather stopped further construction, and in midwinter we prepared to move into the still unfinished new house. Even though it only had a few boards for a ceiling, to me it was the loveliest palace in the world. I was overwhelmed with joy at the prospect of bringing my family into such spacious quarters.

I was expecting my fifth child soon, and with the growing children becoming more and more active we just had to have more room. Indeed, overcrowding, particularly of active children, was the cause of many accidents, some of which brought injury, and others were nearly fatal.

How well I recall one particular incident. One day shortly after my third daughter, Bessie, was born and while we were still living in the shack, I went outside to feed the cattle and our few remaining chickens. My outside chores finished, I returned to the shack and upon opening the door my eyes beheld a dreadful sight. Hannah was shaking violently, and as I stared in stunned disbelief her eyes glazed and turned up into her head. I grabbed the water bucket but even as I dashed the water over her I felt my knees buckling. With a great effort I literally threw the unconscious children through the doorway, meanwhile screaming with all the power left in me. Although my mother-in-law's shack was more than a quarter of a mile away, she heard my desperate shrieking, and immediately started for us. She found me unconscious with my arms around my children. We were all more dead than alive. The baby, Bessie, was so far gone that my mother-in-law could not revive her. When consciousness returned to me, all my in-laws were there. They were working on Bessie trying, but failing, to find a sign of life in the infant. The first words I heard were that the child was dead. That awful moment is one which I will never forget. I tried to go to my poor baby but they held me back. I fainted again, but now the baby began to show signs of life, and when I recovered I was told that all the children were living after all. Whereupon I fainted again, this time from the emotion of joy and thankfulness. This nearly fatal disaster was caused by smoke and gas inhalation from the stove. We had mainly wet wood to burn at this time and the shack was always smoky. The children and I were all sick for a week or so, unable to keep food down.

Although, in winter especially, the stove sustained our lives, it was at the same time always a source of danger. It was my habit to get up at four in the morning, and upon rising to build a fire in the stove and then attend to my cold and wet babies. In the early years particularly, we could not afford to keep the fire going through the night although often the temperature fell to thirty and forty degrees below zero in winter. Usually I would start the fire with dried cow dung. One morning, having completed these first chores, I went to the barn to feed the chickens and cows. I suddenly felt a strong sense of disquiet. I hurried back to the shack. The girls, Minnie and Hannah, had closed the draft in the stove chimney and the place was full of smoke from the smoldering dung. The girls were hovering over the stove apparently trying to stir up the fire. At the moment I entered the room, Minnie's hair which was long and curly caught fire. Thank God for the intuition that had hurried me back to the children. Although I quickly smothered the flames, Minnie suffered serious burns on her face and hands.

Yet another of these tragic accidents occurred when Minnie was two years old and Hannah was five months. I had planned to whitewash this morning, and in preparation I built up the fire and then cleared everything away from the walls to give me operating room. Everything, and the children as well, had to be pushed into the center of the room toward the stove. No sooner had I begun to work than I heard terrible screams coming from both children. Turning, I beheld a horrifying sight. Hannah was lying on the hot stove with her hands

79

Left to right: Abraham, Elizabeth, Rachel Bella, and
Jack (Isaac). Devils Lake, circa 1904-1905.

pressed against the top. I reached her in one mad leap, but her
hands were badly burned. I snatched the poor child to me and
ran to my mother-in-law's place. She advised applying beaten
eggs to the burns. I had no eggs but I was desperate to help my
child. I ran to the field where Abe was working, and he ran to
the nearest neighbor, over five miles distant, for eggs. This was
the poor child's second dreadful experience with burns from
the stove. She had only just recovered from the burn to her
elbow suffered at the time of her birth.

A later daughter, Elizabeth, was also severely burned on her
neck and arm with hot coffee. She carries the scars to this day.

80

Now established in the new house, we slowly began to rebuild our fortunes so thoroughly battered by the great hailstorm. The following year we brought in a fine wheat crop and made progress in other ways as well. We were experienced now and began to feel a growing sense of relationship with the land. We no longer thought of ourselves as strangers in an alien environment but rather as permanent, responsible citizens.

Even though we still endured many hardships and disadvantages, in other ways we were progressing toward a more civilized life. The year after Abe built our home he and Charlie were able to purchase some furniture in town, which they divided. For a long time I felt I must be dreaming to actually have real furniture.

Elizabeth was born to us on a day in November so unbearably cold that we could not keep the house warm. My children huddled about me and I couldn't fully undress, but I attended to my chore.

Although we were increasingly comfortable on the land, we were always aware of our vulnerability to the elements. We had learned only too well about unrelenting cold, so damaging to body and spirit. We knew firsthand about savage storms which could in a matter of minutes destroy the hard-won fruits of years of labor and deprivation.

The great plains, so sparsely populated, spawned fierce cyclones which swept across the prairie with little to stop them. In the hot summers, great whirling winds drove across the flat land and with no obstruction to break them up soon formed into cyclones.

One summer day our immediate area was struck by such a storm. Fortunately I saw the black cone approaching and had time to gather the children into the cellar which served as our storm shelter. Abe was in the field, and I could only hope that he would find some kind of shelter too.

81

As the children and I sat at the bottom of the steps, we were suddenly joined by a large lizard. We had never seen such an animal before and were petrified with fear of it. Even so, as the roaring of the storm came closer, we had no choice but to go into the deepest and darkest part of the cellar, closely accompanied by our unwelcome guest. I would have preferred to sit on the bottom of the cellar steps, but since they were attached to the house floor, if the cyclone carried away the house, the steps would have gone with it. There we sat in the dark, more afraid, if possible, of the lizard than of the storm.

The cyclone missed the house, but the aftermath of it was almost as bad with fearfully high winds and rains as heavy as though the clouds had burst. When the worst of it had passed the ground was flooded as far as I could see.

Abe was nowhere in sight and my apprehension mounted by the second. But soon, in the distance, I saw a figure approaching. Even knowing that it must be Abe, I didn't recognize him so changed was his appearance. With the cyclone almost upon him, he told me, he unharnessed the two horses we had acquired to follow their own instincts for survival. Abe then burrowed into the ground as hard as he could, even burying his face in the wet soil, in the hope that he would not be carried away by the great wind.

I ran to meet him and, both covered with mud, we held one another closely, crying and laughing at the same time. After this experience, I was always on the alert when the sky suddenly clouded over, ready to take the children into the cellar, lizard notwithstanding.

During another storm lightning struck the chicken coop, killing almost the entire flock. The stench of the dead chickens remained intolerable until we found and disposed of the last of them. Soon after Abe installed lightning rods on the coop, the barn, and the house.

82

My seventh child, a son, Alec, was born in April 1907. I had given birth to too many children under harsh and primitive conditions, and my abused body responded poorly to this new demand. After the delivery I fainted many times and became progressively weaker. After the last faint, I awoke to the sound of all the children screaming at the top of their voices. I saw also that Abe sat crying loudly at the side of the bed. I observed this scene as though from another world, and feeling that I did not want to add to the noise I fell into a deep sleep.

I was ill for a long time after Alec's birth but I did not stay in bed very long. The demands of our rigorous life left little tolerance for sickness. My duties awaited only me and could not be put off on others. My children needed me and other matters required my attention as well. True, we hired a man at this time, but to me he was really an added burden. Although he helped me milk the cows, I had to cook for him and wash his clothes. I would gladly have done without him but I knew that he was of help to Abe who labored daily from dawn to dark, harder than any man should.

I came face-to-face with the grim reaper next winter when I was well into my next pregnancy. It seemed that many of our family's emergencies occurred during stormy weather, particularly in the winter months, and this time was no exception. It began early on a Friday morning during a furious blizzard with sleet and snow. I became suddenly ill and shortly began to hemorrhage heavily. It was evident that my condition was very serious, and worsening rapidly. I needed medical help quickly, and it was hastily decided that Abe should stand by me, while Charlie would attempt to get through the storm to town to bring the doctor to me. He left immediately.

I bled throughout the night, and in the dim light of early morning it came to me with clarity that I was close to death. All through the day my mother-in-law tried to slow the bleeding by heaping snow on my stomach. By evening I was more dead than alive, and then, unexpectedly, the doctor was there.

I have been critical many times in this accounting of Charlie's actions and values, and I do not retract anything I have said. But we all at times rise above our usual limitations and on this occasion Charlie was truly heroic. It is probable that his courageous action saved my life. He almost lost his own life fighting through the blizzard, but he kept driving without letup and made the trip in record time, less than two full days and under terrible conditions.

The doctor, having examined me, announced that I was less than two hours from death. My fever was very high and I had lost so much blood, but I was beyond pain, that is, until the doctor removed the fetus. Then, even in my enfeebled state, my screams of pain reached through the raging storm to high heaven.

The doctor remained with me through that night and the next as I went from one crisis into another. I was deathly ill for a week, and after I could hardly stand on my feet.

In thinking about this experience, I was happy that I did not have this child and I felt a growing revolt against bearing more children. But nature, especially on the prairie, took its course, and within a year I gave birth to another daughter, Ceilia.

Because of the near catastrophe of my last pregnancy, it was decided that I should go to town for this delivery under the doctor's supervision. Ceilia's birth [1911] was normal, but it left me sick and weak and I had to stay in town for two weeks before I could attempt the trip back home. I was terribly worried about my family. I had left my eldest daughter Minnie, now barely fifteen years old, in charge of the family, and I knew what a tough challenge she faced. She was herself hardly more than a child, but when I returned I found that this little substitute mother had done a good job and she

continued to be invaluable to me in my nervous and exhausted state.

I had recovered my strength by the following spring, but the
new baby seemed not quite right. She was cranky and uncomfortable all through the summer and I didn't know what to do
to relieve her distress.

When she was seven months old, her health, delicate since
birth, took a turn for the worse. She developed a high fever and
could not urinate. She weakened visibly and was unable to eat
or sleep and, finally, even to cry. I tried all the grandmother
remedies without success. Nothing seemed to help.

It was threshing time and a hard decision had to be made.
Should Abe leave the threshing to take the little girl to town?
We decided to try to wait a few days until the threshing was
finished, at which time we took the poor child to the doctor in
town, but he had no idea of what ailed her or what treatment
to recommend. He was typical of the transient frontier doctors
of this time who were more qualified to treat pigs than people.

Ceil recovered from the acute attack of illness but she
remained small and thin and wore a pained expression. She
neither talked nor walked until she was thirteen months old.
When she did take her first halting steps, my happiness at
seeing her walk quickly turned to dismay as I saw that she
limped badly. It broke my heart to see that thin little girl
walking so painfully, but all we could do about it, it seemed,
was to worry.

By 1910 we had succeeded in our endeavors. The farm was
prosperous and many times the size of the original claims.[38]
Abe was also buying and breaking wild horses, an occupation
which earned him numerous injuries. We were now prominent and respected throughout North Dakota.

Our home became the center for all the Jewish holiday
celebrations. Jewish farmers came from far and near to gather

Abraham and Rachel Bella sit in the sulky; Hannah, Minnie,
and a woman identified as "Monee" stand to the side.

at our home for these occasions, some traveling for days by
horse and buggy and by horseback. These were wonderful and
festive events. Everyone stayed for as long as the holiday
lasted. We put up tents for the visiting children's sleeping
quarters, and in the house sleepers occupied all the chairs and
covered the floors.

Our house lights now were kerosene powered. The fuel was
forced into a tank with a bicycle pump and then to light
fixtures which were made with cloth mantles. The mantles
gave off an intense white light, and travelers on the prairie
oriented themselves by this beacon, while to approaching
guests it signaled that their haven was near. Another benefit of
our distinctive lights was to keep bothersome wild animals
from our door and the chicken coop.

We had plenty of food now. Each late fall now, the *shochet*
paid us a visit for the coming winter. The dressed animals were

stored in the barn which served as our winter freezer. What a contrast to the slow starvation of the early winters.

Our family was now so large, and guests so numerous and frequent, that Abe was inspired to devise an apparatus to ease the distribution of food at meal times. He drove an iron shaft into the center of the table which acted as an axle upon which revolved a huge wagon wheel covered with a board face. This enormous lazy susan, loaded with food, was helpful in reducing the confusion and delay caused by many hungry people passing and reaching for the various dishes. During meals the wheel was always in motion, and one needed only to wait a moment or two to find the desired food before him.

Now Abe, deprived of educational opportunity during his younger years, was more able to satisfy his hunger for knowledge. Despite his intolerably long hours of labor he became an avid reader of everything in print he could get his hands on.[39] He became qualified to speak with authority on many subjects and he put his learning to work, helping in the development of the area in many respects. He introduced a number of improvements in agricultural practices and marketing.

The first school board in the area was organized largely through his efforts and he served on it with distinction. He was blessed with vision and could visualize a school system far beyond the first, one-room, one-teacher school which my older children attended.

His accomplishments were widely recognized, and he received personal letters of commendation from two presidents of the United States, William Taft and Woodrow Wilson.

Our first schoolhouse was a simple one-room building much like the prairie shacks of the early days.[40] It served four families. In the winter the teacher slept in the schoolhouse, and often the children arriving there in the morning would

87

Students of the Victoria School, circa 1912. Rachel Bella and
Abraham Calof's children are Alec (first row, fourth from the
left); Elizabeth (first row, far right); Isaac (Jack) (second row, far
left); Minnie (second row, fourth from the left); and Moses (Mac)
(third row, far right, with face partially obscured). Charlie and
Faga's children are Max (second row, third from the left); Oscar
(third row, far left); and Lilly (third row, third from the left).
The teacher, Katie Kabker, is at the right end of the second row.

find her still asleep. Under these circumstances the school day
began with a recess while the teacher dressed and cooked her
breakfast. When a student finished his current "reader" book,
he was promoted to the next grade.

Although, in general, the conditions of our lives now bore
little semblance to the circumstances we endured in the early
days on the land, for me there was to be one further experience
reminiscent of those hard times.

Despite my aversion to bearing more children, I gave birth
to my final child, a son, Jacob, in March 1912. Because of the
complications of my last pregnancies, I thought it best to

88

deliver the child in town, where hopefully I would have medical help available to me. I was accompanied by my eldest and youngest daughters, Minnie and Ceil.

The conditions of the confinement in some ways were even worse than the past ones on the farm. The only lodging we could find to rent was an empty store located under a roller skating rink. The furniture consisted of a bed and a stove, and the noise and dust from above were terrible. What an awful place to bring a child into the world.

Jake weighed almost thirteen pounds at birth and my agony in giving him life was great. The doctor who was to attend me was named Cox. He wasn't exactly a friendly type, but he was all that was available. He was almost completely drunk most of the time and totally drunk the rest of the time. When my labor started he was too intoxicated to come to me, but instead sent a boy with some big pills which made me deathly ill. This terrible man was well-known in the area. It was rumored that because of his drunkenness and ignorance he caused the deaths of many a pioneer mother.

I never fully recovered from the abuses of this and my previous deliveries, and years later when I lived in St. Paul, Minnesota, I underwent surgery to repair my torn insides, but without favorable result.

Though we continued to improve the farm and its yield, there were many painful setbacks and we were never completely free of fear. The weather was largely unpredictable. Hailstorms could destroy most or all of a crop in a few minutes. Excessive rain rusted the wheat and made it useless, while lack of rain turned crops to dust.

The other two families eventually failed in their efforts to permanently establish themselves on the land. Charlie and his family left North Dakota, and Abe's father and mother continued to spend the winters with us, each time supposedly the last. It was always referred to as a temporary arrangement, but

89

it persisted for eighteen years. In the later years Abe's mother became our permanent guest, my father-in-law having died. Their son, Moe [Moses], married and left for other adventures.

Now at age sixty, and thinking back through this history, I feel a satisfying pride in myself. I stood shoulder-to-shoulder with my husband and proved capable in meeting the challenges which so many of the settlers failed to survive. I took life as it was presented to me and then did my best to improve it.

Although I withstood privation well, having been introduced to it at a very early age, I must confess that the one hardship which was always unacceptable to me through the formative years was the lack of privacy. For many months of each of those years Abe and I had to find our privacy on the open prairie, and even in later years we had to hold our personal conversations in the barn.

In those precarious winters of the first years when so many people, and animals as well, huddled together in a tiny space, my yearning was not for a larger shack but rather for the dignity of privacy.

My resentment of this imposition grew with each succeeding year and finally it became a serious issue between Abe and me. In all other risks and discomforts our cause was a common one, but in this one matter I became more unwilling to compromise with each passing year.

The year 1917 was one of sober reflection and decision for Abe and me. In many ways we were comfortable and satisfied. We could look back with pride on our accomplishments. We had come as raw immigrants without resources or training to a stark wilderness in a strange country, and we tamed the land and made it fit for humans. We had earned the respect and friendship of many.

Laughter came easier now, and the memories of past bitter experiences had softened with age, but time and privation had

90

taken their toll. Abe now suffered greatly with rheumatism and my own health was impaired. We realized that the rigors of the farming life were too much for us to endure longer, that it was time to move on to another kind of life.

I had traveled a long and often torturous way from the little *shtetl* [town or Jewish community] in Russia where I was born. It wasn't an easy road by any means, but if you love the living of life you must know the journey was well worth it.

Notes

1. Belaya Tserkov is located on the Res River about fifty kilometers south of Kiev in Ukraine. The location of "Chvedkifka" cannot be established and no additional relevant family history exists. There is a small town south of Belaya Tserkov, now called Charaievka, which might be the place mentioned in the narrative.

2. Eda Velvel Cohen was a religious leader of the local Orthodox community. Marrying beneath the family's caste would violate norms related to their social status and, in particular, the family's linkage to the *Kohanim* (religious leaders). Rachel Bella Calof's son, Jacob, recalls her proudly referring to herself as a *Bas Kohena*, a title from biblical times meaning "daughter of a priest."

3. Each of these practices is of course taboo for religious Orthodox Jews. Ashkenazic (eastern and central European) Orthodox women were expected to cut their hair and wear a *sheitel* (wig) after marriage, to keep kosher dietary laws that include strict prohibitions against mixing meat or meat-containing foods with milk or milk-containing foods, to respect prohibitions against all forms of work (including cooking and lighting fires) on the Sabbath, and to send their children to religious schools.

4. Eighteen years is an important watershed age; the Mishnah (the first division of the Talmud, which contains rabbinic interpretations of biblical laws) suggests it as the most appropriate age for marriage.

Many young women at that time in the Pale of Settlement married before reaching their eighteenth birthday.

5. Since this is the first mention of a member of the Calof family, some relationships should here be explained. Chaya (later "Ida") is the sister of Abraham, Savol (later "Charlie"), and Moses. Their parents are Solomon and Charadh (Myers). Family members differed in transliterations of their last name into English. Solomon, Charadh, and Charlie typically used Kalov, Abraham preferred Calof, and his brother Moses favored Kalof. Rachel Bella Calof's variable use of given names versus designation by family relationships is an important stylistic feature of her account. She refers to some individuals (e.g., her mother-in-law) only by their kinship relationships to other characters in the narrative.

6. One of these "cities" may have been Steblev, the childhood home of two first cousins, Maier and Leib Calof, who at that time were already homesteaders in the Devils Lake area.

7. Steerage passage was the cheapest fare available. It typically connoted communal and unvented bunking areas in the lower and rear portions of the ship near the engines and rudder.

8. According to family members, Rachel Bella never again saw any of her siblings. The family possesses three posed photographs identified as the families of her brothers and sister, but no one knows anything of their lives or fates.

9. Little is known about Abraham's experiences in the United States between the time of his emigration with his brother Charlie in 1891 and Rachel Bella Kahn's arrival in 1894. There is no indication that Abraham spent any time on farms, although he may have visited his two cousins already settled in the Devils Lake area. Abraham likely spent his three years living and working in New York to raise funds for his family's passage.

10. This passage joins together family members who actually had arrived in two distinct emigrations. Abraham, Charlie, Doba, and Sarah came in 1891 and the remainder of the Kalov family emigrated in 1894.

Doba and Sarah Zaslavsky were related to Abraham through the common link of his maternal grandmother. The two sisters came to the United States under the sponsorship of an arranged marriage to

Maier and Leib Calof, Abraham's first cousins. The two sisters were thus distantly related to their spouses and to Abraham through marriage. The orchestrated process that brought these four individuals together in North Dakota has similarities to the union of Rachel Bella and Abraham Calof. See Maier Calof, *Miracles of the Lives of Maier and Doba Calof* (privately printed, 1941).

11. The "binders" are horse-pulled, mechanical reapers that cut standing grain, tied it into bundles, and then deposited them back on the ground. The bundles had to be collected and formed into standing formations ("shocks") of seven to twelve bundles in order to allow the grain to dry before threshing. Normally, one man was hard-pressed to shock behind a single binder.

12. The references to settling on state land are difficult to understand. They could refer to the school sections on which no claims could be filed or land withheld from settlement by the government for railroad grants or other planned enterprises.

13. The location of the original claim is not known. The second homestead claim that became the Calof farm is located in Overland Township (Section 29 of Township 157 North, Range 62 West).

14. The purpose of fasting before the wedding is to atone, as on Yom Kippur, for past sins and to allow the married pair to begin their life together free from the past. The reference to "praying with tears" to her dead parent invokes two wedding customs: recitation of memorial prayers before the wedding ceremony and lamentation as a symbolic reminder of the destruction of Jerusalem.

15. That the day was "coming to a close" is important because they were married on Friday, November 8, 1894, and they needed to complete the wedding ceremony before sunset and the beginning of the Sabbath. The Calof family likely would have followed Jewish custom prohibiting marriages during the Sabbath period.

16. This man may have been Benjamin Greenberg, a local Jewish farmer and justice of the peace.

17. The flour sack (and later a handkerchief) serves as a veil. The importance of the wedding veil in Judaism typically relates to its symbolic role in marking a transition from single to married status and, less often, to warding off evil spirits.

93

18. The *huppah* (wedding canopy) marks off a symbolic marriage area spatially separated from the everyday world and hence contributes to the construction of a new space (and status) for husband and wife.

19. The next several pages of the narrative contain many references to folk beliefs and customs surrounding protection of newborns from baby-stealing devils. Many of these practices, including the use of religious artifacts (e.g., prayer books) and metal (e.g., knives), are found among diverse cultural groups. For discussions of Jewish traditions associated with babies and devils, see Theodore H. Gaster, *The Holy and the Profane: Evolution of Jewish Folkways* (New York: William Sloane, 1955), pp. 3-44; Raphael Patai, *On Jewish Folklore* (Detroit: Wayne State University Press, 1983), pp. 337-443, and "Folk Customs and Charms Relating to Birth," *Talpoith* 4 (1953-54): 226-68, 686-705; Joshua Trachtenberg, *The Devil and the Jews* (New Haven: Yale University Press, 1943); and Chaim Schauss, "The Birth of a Jewish Child," *Yivo Bleter* 17 (1941): 47-63.

20. Rachel Bella Calof's mother-in-law likely interpreted the lack of stars in the sky as meaning the Sabbath was still not over and thus a fire could not be started to heat the milk. The tone of the passage also suggests, however, that the author knew of this interpretation and, in keeping with Jewish law, believed the health of the child to be more important than the keeping of Sabbath rules.

21. Rachel Bella Calof's mother-in-law, who was so adamant about certain Jewish customs, appears to be preparing a meal that violates the central *kashrut* dietary prohibition against mixing milk and meat. This inconsistency remains unexplained; it may be a simple question of memory.

22. The knife may have been largely intended as a weapon with which to fight the devils. Although there is no description of the knife itself, the fact that it is a metal implement may also be significant. Iron, steel, and other metals are considered effective amulets for scaring off devils in traditional Jewish and other belief systems. Metals and metal implements were at one time common throughout Europe to keep various demons and fairy creatures from stealing human babies.

23. The prohibition against lighting a fire remains in force because the Sabbath period is not yet ended.

24. The act of milking a cow might appear to violate Sabbath prohibitions against work and most kinds of physical exertion. In this case, milking is permitted in order to treat Rachel Bella Calof's illness and protect her life as well as to maintain the health of the cow.

25. According to Orthodox tradition, a woman who has just given birth is *niddah* (unclean) due to the presence of blood. The period of separation in Rachel Bella Calof's case is not given. Formal periods of sexual abstinence could range from seven days for the birth of a boy to eighty days for a girl. The biblical ordinances are found in Leviticus 12:1-8.

26. It is impossible to know which religious "law" is referred to in the warnings of Rachel Bella's mother-in-law. Traditional grounds for divorce center around rabbinical interpretations of *ervat davar* (matters of indecency) as described in Deuteronomy 24:1 and could include provisions based on mental illness. For an interesting contemporary discussion of rabbinic interpretations, see Rachel Biale, *Women and Jewish Law: An Exploration of Women's Issues in Halakhic Sources* (New York: Schocken, 1984), pp. 70-101.

27. Family members identify this unnamed friend as Doba Calof, wife of Maier Calof.

28. Rachel Bella Calof may be referring to the traditional garment known as the *tachrichim* (shrouds) in which the dead are wrapped before burial. As her story suggests, white is the preferred color of the cloth.

29. To maintain the laws of the *kashrut* (dietary laws), a trained *shochet* or ritual slaughterer familiar with the code of the *Shulchan Aruch* would be necessary for this task.

30. Pigs are not considered kosher due to the prohibition of eating warm-blooded animals that do not have a parted or cloven hoof and that do not regurgitate their food (chew their cud). The biblical basis for this prohibition is in Deuteronomy 14:3-8.

31. Fort Totten was the closest large reservation, though it was located on the south side of Devils Lake.

32. According to the Bible, the ritual of circumcision was insti-

tuted at the time of Abraham. Rachel Bella Calof's use of the phrase "wonderful ceremony of the Covenant" is an apt description of this rite of passage marking the baby's admission into the communal covenant both with God and within the social community.

33. Certain parts of kosher animals are not edible, including the fat around various organs, the sciatic nerve, and connected tendons in the hindquarter. Although the sciatic nerve and tendons could be removed (a process called *treibering*), this practice is rarely done by Ashkenazic Jews in the United States.

34. The narrative does not indicate why the *shochet* judged the meat as not kosher. The laws of the *kashrut* include both the *shehitah* (slaughtering) and an examination of the organs of the slaughtered animal. Any variety of discoveries (e.g., disease, infection, injury, or physical abnormality) during this second phase can cause the *shochet* to declare the animal as *traif*.

35. The *shochet* here is upholding the most basic of all laws—the preservation of human life. There are a variety of allowable exceptions to Jewish customs and prohibitions in cases where upholding a norm in a particular social context threatens human health and safety.

36. The most likely reason for the *shochet's* instruction to use a great deal of salt relates to the absolute prohibition of eating blood in any form. Salt is the best method for drawing all the remaining blood from the meat and is a critical part of *kashering* (preparing meat prior to cooking). Many folk belief systems include salt as a special protector against evil and disease.

37. Perhaps this was necessary because the Calofs farmed adjoining farmsteads with no fences to indicate property lines.

38. According to the Ramsey County plat book of 1909, Abraham Calof owned 360 acres in Sections 29, 30, and 32 of Overland Township. He also co-owned some land in partnership with his brother Charlie, including 120 acres of school section land they sold in 1910.

39. In a letter to the editor of the *Edmore Herald News* printed on December 20, 1905, Abraham described a more formal attempt to organize his spare time for intellectual and social ends:

As farmers, we always try to pass our spare time in a pleasant and progressive way. This means we have always the intention to give our life the color and shape of city people. Accordingly, we five families, living close to one another, have organized a society called "The Farmers' Sociability."

Here are the principal rules for the new organization. All the members are divided into three classes, according to ages from ten to fifteen and older. The committee, which consists of a representative from each class, has to make up a program for every evening. Literature, science, debates, oratory, music, and dances will make up the programs.

We are all in full hopes that the new style of sociability will be of benefit to every one of our members and that we and our children will gladly participate in the new organization which has the sociability and scientific platforms.

40. In the early 1900s, the older Calof children attended Victoria School, located in Section 20 and close to the Calof farm in Overland Township.

EPILOGUE

Jacob Calof

The philosophies of my mother, Rachel Bella Calof, were simple and profound and were formulated early in life. From them she evolved attitudes and principles that guided and sustained her in all of her travails and triumphs. Having once established her personal code for living, she never deviated from it.

Basic to her convictions was an appreciation that she had been favored with the greatest of all possible endowments, that of life itself. Early on, she resolved to live that life to the fullest potential that circumstances would allow.

Although without formal education, she was blessed with a keen intuitive intelligence and a talent for expression in the written word. I remember that she seemed always to have about her an air of quiet expectation.

Ever ready to help others in any way she could, she seldom offered advice unless asked. Her demeanor was calm and sweet, and though readily accessible, she was essentially a very private person.

She seldom spoke of the past, but in the times when I observed her in those rare moments of introspection and reverie, I understood full well that this was private property, no trespassing permitted. I believe that having been denied privacy for most of her years, she regarded the

Rachel Bella and Abraham in St. Paul,
circa 1925–1930.

occasional opportunity for self-communion as one of the most prized
attainments, finally, of her life.

Together with their entire brood of nine and my father's mother, my
parents left the farm and North Dakota in 1917. They moved to St. Paul,
Minnesota, where my father bought and operated a grocery store. This
venture failed after a year or two, and the rest of his working career was
as a dry goods salesman. He developed a door-to-door clientele, initially
carrying his inventory on the back of a bicycle; later, becoming more
successful, he conducted his business from the back seat of an automobile. At about the same time, most of the remaining Calofs in North
Dakota moved also to St. Paul and were absorbed into the city in prosaic
occupations and pursuits.

Now entering once again a radically different life as city dwellers, so

Rachel Bella Calof, near 70,
Seattle, 1945.

alien from that of their past twenty-some years, the marriage of Rachel
Bella and Abraham continued much as before with trust and dependence on one another in adapting to yet another new world.

Subtly, however, as the great prior demands upon their energies for
the basics of existence eased, each at last found opportunity, so long
denied, for individual expression. With the development of their new-
found personal freedom, their bond of mutuality began to erode,
replaced more and more by divergent views and activities. The ties of
common danger and uncertainty, dependence on each other's skills, and
shared emotional support seemed no longer essential in their relationship. Slowly, then, they began to drift apart.

Abraham's interests tended primarily to causes in education and local
politics, but leaning ever to the international arena. Rachel Bella's calling

remained always faithful to the immediate community of her large family and showed itself in services to local society.

As a courtesy to Abraham, she also played hostess to a growing crowd of itinerant lecturers, intellectuals, and revolutionaries who brought their large viewpoints and even larger appetites to her table. She treated this assortment of visionaries with humor and tolerance, and occasionally she found merit in some opinions, but by and large she viewed them as ineffectuals.

Increasingly my parents strayed from each other. Their later visits to children who had married and moved away were always done by each of them alone. Yet always these two decent and excellent people continued to treat one another with consideration, respect, and honesty.

Long after my mother's death, my sister Elizabeth presented me with two studio photographs made in Russia of two family groups. She understood these to be pictures of our mother's sister and one brother and their families. So far as I know, though, my mother never had further contact with her siblings after she embarked upon her voyage to America.

In her later life, Rachel Bella developed serious health problems, a great number of which had been caused by her many childbirths unattended and under primitive conditions. Yet she seldom complained and she never surrendered to her illnesses. She seemed always undaunted, ever cheerful, and in repose her expression was always one of that calm anticipation that I knew so well and valued so much.

In her seventy-second year her right leg was amputated, and although urged to accept life in a wheelchair, she would have none of that. She did all that was required to fit her with an artificial limb, and she stayed mobile for all but the final day of her life.

Once, soon after she lost her leg, when in her helplessness I carried her to my automobile, I saw tears in her eyes. That heartbreaking remembrance remains with me, for it was the only time I ever knew her to cry.

The most vivid memory I treasure of her was the lovely picture she presented wearing her immaculate white apron over her best dress in her warm, spotless house, making her blessing over the Sabbath candles each Friday evening. How noble and regal she looked.

Her honorable and distinguished life ended in Seattle, Washington, at the age of seventy-six.

BELLEVUE, WASHINGTON

JEWISH FARM SETTLEMENTS IN AMERICA'S HEARTLAND

J. Sanford Rikoon

The individuals and families who left Russia and eastern Europe and attempted to settle on Heartland farms did not differ in many respects from the majority of their fellow immigrants who resided in places like New York or Chicago. There is thus no need to restate existing discussions on the factors that caused Jews to leave the Old World, the areas they left, how they made their way to the United States, or the cultural and social baggage they carried across the ocean. What sets Rachel Bella Calof, the Calof family, and their Devils Lake neighbors apart from the bulk of Jewish immigrants was their participation in a social movement that viewed Heartland farming as an appropriate economic and social alternative for Jewish immigrants. To place Rachel Bella's account into historical and social contexts, this essay is intended to introduce readers to Jewish settlement in the rural Heartland and, in particular, to the patterns of movement to homesteads and communities in North Dakota near the time of her arrival.

Jewish Settlement on Heartland Farms

Almost all Jewish families attempting to farm in the Heartland began their efforts between 1880 and 1930 as part of one of three major initiatives. The Calof family experience falls under the earliest, a movement comprising individual families and small groups who opted to develop government and railroad lands in frontier regions. Most of this activity occurred in North and South Dakota between 1880 and 1910, although early efforts also developed on cutover lands in Wisconsin and Michigan and railroad tracts and prairie areas from Illinois to western Kansas and Nebraska. The second initiative began around 1900 and continued through the Depression era. The families in this movement also favored individual farmsteads but preferred to purchase already-developed farms in areas close to midwestern urban areas with strong Jewish congregations. The largest settlement areas in this phase occurred in southwestern Michigan and the Geneva region east of Cleveland.

Communal endeavors distinguish the final pattern of Jewish farm settlement. Although efforts of this nature occurred periodically between 1880 and 1940, the aggregate number of individuals involved totaled less than 10 percent of the overall Heartland Jewish farm population. Only rarely did any formalized cooperative ventures persevere with any strength for more than three years.[2] The basis for collective actions ranged from agrarian doctrines conceived during the period of European Jewish enlightenment to socialist precepts formulated in American urban centers. The earliest efforts derived from nineteenth-century Russian *maskalim* (enlightened ones), some of whom banded together in the *Am Olam* (Eternal People) movement in the 1880s and moved to colonies from New Jersey to Oregon, including South Dakota.[3] The last communalist settlement was organized under a socialist plan by Joseph J. Cohen, former editor of the *Freie-Arbeiter Shtimme*, the Yiddish anarchist weekly. The colonists titled their Depression era effort the Sunrise Co-operative Farm Community, and the former easterners toiled for approximately three years near Alicia, Michigan.[4]

Beyond the skeleton outlines of settlement it is difficult to retrieve many of those basic facts we assume are necessary to describe adequately a chapter of Jewish-American social history. For example, we have tremendous problems even knowing how many individuals or families joined in this movement. The number between 1880 and 1940 in the Heartland may be around 8,000 people, but this is a conservative figure that perhaps greatly underestimates the total. Leonard Robinson, the general manager of the Jewish Agricultural and Industrial Aid Society, reported in 1912 that his group had contact with over 3,400 persons in midwestern states. This figure was not comprehensive, Robinson noted, representing "not much more than half" of the Jewish farm population.[5] Among the problems facing anyone who would count the settlers is that no agency ever undertook a religious census of farmers during the time of early Jewish settlement. More importantly, the farm experience was usually a rather ephemeral one, lasting between two and five years for most settlers. Thus families could easily have been in and out of an area before a census taker ever visited their farm or before their existence ever became known to one of the Jewish agencies so integral to the movement.

Other aspects of the movement are less mysterious. Virtually all farm settlers were part of the great movement of people fleeing their homes in the Russian Pale of Settlement[6] and eastern Europe during the last two decades of the nineteenth century and first decade of the twentieth century. Although there had been occasional German Jewish farmers in the Heartland prior to this time, for the most part these were rather isolated efforts that never took on the attributes of a social movement.[7] Some of the German Jewish farmers became quite successful in their operations, but their progress had little impact on the interests or demography of immigrant German Jews in general.

The more widespread participation of Russian and eastern European Jews in agriculture was not simply a product of their overwhelming numbers. The best clues to their decisions are their socioeconomic standing and their symbolic construction of a rural landscape promising dramatic economic and, to lesser extent, social improvement in their lives. The people who settled on farms were generally poor when they moved to the countryside. They either reached the United States with little money or dropped to near poverty levels after their arrival in eastern or midwestern cities where they found it immensely difficult to do more than just survive. Issues of class and place, of course, often overlap. Jewish life in urban ghetto areas, the initial residence of most immigrants of this period, is well documented. With little opportunity for the types of work or wages that might have allowed improvement in their lives, some men (and it was almost always a male decision to leave the community for the farm) turned their visions to the countryside and the farm. Only in rare cases did any middle- or upper-class Russian Jews become active participants, in large part because they did not need to pursue alternative lifestyles in order to profit under existing dominant economic systems. For some of their poorer countrymen, though, the farm represented social and economic freedom.

And it was on the level of symbol that most would-be farmers conceived their future lives in rural areas. Few Jewish immigrants had been farmers in the Old World and almost none had any agricultural experience in the United States before the move to a homestead or a purchased farm in the Heartland. The lack of farming background was partly a product of prohibitions against rural land ownership in many of the Old World areas from which they had emigrated. Further, most newcomers and urban dwellers had little sense of the realities of Heartland farming. While some immigrants undoubtedly arrived with the intention of settling on the land, most were unaware of the opportunities that existed. There were no widely known Jewish rural areas of the United States. The land agents, railroad companies, and real estate entrepreneurs who peddled U.S. farming in some Old World areas virtually ignored potential Jewish immigrants.[8] As the Jewish farm movement began in the United States, letters from family members in the New World and occasional news of Jewish farming efforts in the Old World Jewish press did motivate some immigration directly to rural areas, although the numbers were relatively small.[9]

The amount and direction of agrarian idealism motivating farm settlement are difficult to untangle and unquestionably varied among individuals. Certainly some of the organized communal efforts of the *Am Olam* and the plans of colony architects in the United States reflect a deep impact of nineteenth-century movements founded on odd mixtures of romantic, socialist, and communalist utopian thinking. Most immigrants, not surprisingly, have left little record or evidence attributing their decisions to farm to any conceptual bases. But we should not confuse the lack of an enduring or formally expressed ideal with the absence of a symbolic construct of a personal agrarian-based future. Within the social and economic contexts and constraints dominating the lives of most immigrants, would-be farmers constructed agrarian visions in which farming offered personal independence and freedom.

Notions of independence were linked to envisioning rural landscapes free from the oppression of the Old World and, in many cases, the New World as well. The reminiscences, diaries, and reflections of men describing their move to the farm often use the terms "freedom" or "opportunity" to describe their reasons for entering agriculture. Of all that America represented in the immigrant imagination, the vision of the farm was an improved version. America itself offered relief from pogroms, military service, anti-Semitic rules and regulations, and oppressive governments. The farm, in turn, provided additional escape from factory bosses, crowded apartments, and urban anti-Semitism. Farming promised the opportunity to own land and the chance to work for oneself and for one's own future. The self-sufficient individual farmer captured the imagination of people who viewed agriculture not only as a way to succeed economically, but perhaps more importantly as a means to control their economic destiny. It suggested the right and responsibilities of being your own boss and the possibility of taking a step towards economic well-being. The freedom promised by the farm was grounded in economics, then, but economic opportunity was viewed as inherently related to social values and concerns.

Thoughts of becoming a farmer might well have remained a dream for all but the most adventurous immigrants; most had neither the resources nor the knowledge necessary to take the initial steps toward land-ownership. But for reasons grounded primarily in romanticism and assimilationist ideologies, the idea of a Russian and eastern European immigrant movement to farms found strong backing among some urban community and business leaders, philanthropic agencies, and congregations. These supporters were largely from earlier western and central European immigrant waves. Their idea of the Heartland Jewish farmer stressed that farming was both a viable economic alternative and the means to resolve a number of social and cultural problems associated with new immigrants and expanding urban ghettos. Direct immigrant settlement and urban removal to midwestern farms could relieve city congestion and shrink the size of the ghetto areas. Official proponents also believed that rural life offered a "more sanitary and robust life"[10] than the poverty, disease, and sickness their agencies or congregations associated with ghetto existence. Farm living not only cured the physical body but also promoted social cohesiveness and values by distancing families from the psychic maladies of the city.

Finally, the movement offered an opportunity to relocate the more visibly religious newcomers, who were the overt targets of increasing anti-Semitic attacks and implicit sources of intrareligious conflict and embarrassment. Removal to farms would not only turn immigrants into useful citizens, it would also aid in their Americanization. Before Frederick Jackson Turner espoused his views on the normalizing experience of the frontier, Jewish philanthropies recognized that farming the wilderness would speed the process of transition from visitor/outsider to citizen/insider.

Jewish settlement on Heartland farms would have attracted far fewer participants without the aid of congregational sponsors and philanthropic agricultural societies. Congregational support typically took the form of a one-to-one relationship between an urban patron group and a semiplanned settlement of urban refugees from the congregation's home base. The forms of sustenance were generally start-up monies for the purchase of land, farming equipment, stock, and general supplies. As the sponsored communities languished, their benefactors sent more money, more supplies, an occasional load of kosher meat, and, in some instances, a mentor to instruct the settlers on proper farming methods.

In the case of Cincinnati's Hebrew Union Agricultural Society and the Beersheba, Kansas, colony, the umbilical link stretched close to one thousand miles. Most midwestern city groups, however, located their rural satellite efforts within a more reasonable distance. Among the pairings most notable in scope and length were those of St. Paul and eastern North Dakota, Milwaukee and Arpin, Wisconsin, and Detroit and Bad Axe, Michigan. Some religious or community leaders, including Cincinnati's Isaac Mayer Wise and Milwaukee's Adolph Rich, took it upon themselves to plan the rural colonies,[11] beginning with the selection of the site and the evaluation of prospective settlers. In other cases, groups that had set out on their own and found themselves unprepared for winter or suffering through a variety of hardships appealed to the nearest urban Jewish community for help. Organized congregational support usually lasted no longer than two or three years. The dependent rural communities, typically already on the decline when the assistance ended, usually withered with the withdrawal of support.

Longer-lasting and more widespread assistance for farmers came from two philanthropic groups, the Chicago-based Jewish Agriculturalists' Aid Society of America (JAAS) and, especially, the Jewish Agricultural and Industrial Aid Society (JAIAS) of New York. The Chicago society organized in 1888 and provided farm loans for the next twenty years. Its charter noted the goals to "promote agricultural pursuits among the Jews in general, and to assist and encourage such of the Jewish poor as are able and willing to establish themselves as farmers."[12] The rationale given for this work was fairly typical of most philanthropic and charitable efforts:

> We take the unfortunate out of the overcrowded and sickly ghetto, from the midst of misery and squalor, out into the country where the air is pure and healthful; we change their occupation from a peddler, or laborer, or a tailor, earning perhaps $7.00 a week, into the honorable position of farmer, who may have to rough it for a year or more, but who will soon thereafter be absolutely independent and after a few years be comparatively in good circumstance.[13]

The primary founder and guiding light of JAAS was Abraham R. Levy, rabbi of Congregation B'nai Abraham. The society counted among its chief officers such well-known Chicago philanthropists as Adolph Loeb, Julius Rosenwald, and Judge Hugo Pam. Between 1888 and 1908, JAAS provided settlement loans ranging from $50 to $1,600 to 430 farmers. The majority of its work occurred between 1901 and 1908, during which period the society granted over $100,000 in aid and loans. An analysis of known recipients of JAAS funds reveals efforts to assist both people already on farms who needed help and Chicago families requesting support to leave the city and settle on the land.[14]

JAAS favored a plan of individual family settlement rather than sponsorship of either communalistic endeavors or even loosely knit communities of Jewish farm families. Rabbi Levy defined JAAS's plan as

> Not colonization—settling many families together—with a view to secure religious and social advantages, but the placing of individual families on separate farms, without regard as to the distance to the next Jewish farmer. . . . This principle has proven to be as essential to the success of the undertaking as has the application of *individualism* in every other particular of the work . . . dealing with the would-be Jewish farmer.[15]

From a present perspective, the rhetoric of the JAAS seems naive about the practice of farming and insensitive to the settlers' preference for, as well as the social and cultural importance of, concentrated ethnic settlement. The plan's emphasis on self-reliance and beliefs about dispersed farmsteads reflected its writer's acculturation of dominant values privileging individualism. The rhetoric also suggests a perceived lack of assimilative progress on the part of the new immigrants. According to this worldview, the replication of *shtetl* life in the New World inhibited assimilation by fostering dependency on Old World beliefs and customs. The amount of agricultural expertise among the collective directorship of JAAS was far lower than its level of enthusiasm for farming. In fairness to Rabbi Levy, he worked tirelessly on the part of "would-be Jewish farmers" and each year ventured into North Dakota to chart the successes of his protégés. The testimonies published in JAAS annual reports fairly brim over with zeal and optimism.

JAAS collapsed in 1910 with most of its loans unpaid and previous supporters unwilling to contribute more funds. Leadership of Heartland settlement then rested solely with the Jewish Agricultural and Industrial Aid Society. Precursors of this group actually had been involved in Heartland farm efforts for almost twenty years, thanks to a combination of the interests and financial legacies of Baron Maurice de Hirsch (1831- 96) and agricultural impulses among various early New York philan- thropic associations. With the deterioration of Jewish life in Russia and eastern Europe, the Bavarian-born de Hirsch turned some of his fortune made from European railroad and other financial ventures into organi- zations (especially the *Alliance Israélite Universelle* in Paris) and activities intended both to improve life in Russia and to enhance viable emigration possibilities.[16] By 1890 he had given up on the first hope and focused on the second, which he now recognized included not just removal but also opportunities to make a new start in new places.

Baron de Hirsch founded the Jewish Colonization Association in London in 1891 to aid in emigration movements worldwide and also founded the Baron de Hirsch Fund in New York City specifically to aid Jewish immigrants in the United States.[17] Reflecting their endower's beliefs, both organizations included agricultural settlement as a core goal of resettlement activity.

> My own personal experience has led me to recognize that the Jews have very good ability in agriculture. . . . I have seen this personally in the Jewish agricultural colonies in Turkey. My efforts shall show that the Jews have not lost the agricultural qualities that their forefathers possessed. I shall try to make for them a new home in different lands where, as free farmers on their own soil, they can make themselves useful to the country.[18]

Baron de Hirsch's opinions about farming as a fitting occupation for new immigrants fit perfectly with individual efforts and organizational mandates already being pursued in New York City. In the early 1880s, the Hebrew Emigrant Aid Society, under the leadership of Judge Myer S. Isaacs, contributed funds to the first Heartland farming efforts as well as to colonies in Colorado and New Jersey. Michael Heilprin organized the Montefiore Agricultural Aid Society in New York in 1884 and raised funds for efforts in South Dakota, Oregon, Kansas, and New Jersey. Other New Yorkers who favored agricultural settlement and later became central figures in de Hirsch Fund programs included Oscar S. Straus, Jacob H. Schiff, Julius Goldman, and A. S. Solomons.

During its first decade (1891-1900), the Agriculture and Industry Department of the Baron de Hirsch Fund provided 213 Heartland farm loans and embarked on a rather diverse sampler of other agriculture-related efforts, including a National Agricultural College in Doylestown, Pennsylvania, and experimental colonies in several New Jersey towns. With the hope of being better able to address its rural activities, and with some additional monies from the Jewish Colonization Association, the fund directors created the Jewish Agricultural and Industrial Aid Society (JAIAS) in 1900 as a separate organization. De Hirsch employees (and, perhaps more importantly, the fund's endowers and volunteer directors) had by this time firmly rejected the idea of communal settlements as "impractical schemes . . . merely transferring Jewish Ghettos from large cities to agricultural districts."[19] Their major farm emphases were loans to families seeking to buy existing farms and support of families in the older settlement areas.

JAIAS worked primarily in the East but supported Heartland efforts directly with farm loans and through other agency-sponsored activities. With the demise of the JAAS, the New York agency opened a branch office in Chicago and directed all Midwest operations from that office until 1947. The JAIAS leadership was rather creative in the kinds of assistance gradually added to their programs. For example, they established an agency "Extension Service" six years prior to the formal adoption of a similar system by the United States Department of Agriculture in 1914. The JAIAS also initiated publication of the *Yiddish Farmer* in 1908, a magazine that for over fifty years may have been the only Yiddish-language farm magazine in the world. Other JAIAS programs included a farm labor bureau to provide young men with agricultural experience and a farm credit arm to offer small short-term loans to farmers.[20]

Although Rachel Bella Calof's narrative makes no references to the family's interactions with agricultural societies, her husband, Abraham Calof, and other members of his extended family received loans from both groups. Initial assistance came from the JAAS, which in 1889 provided settlement loans to two of Abraham's first cousins, Maier Calof and John (Leib) Calof. Five years later, Abraham, Saul Calof (Rachel Bella's brother-in-law), Moses Calof (another brother-in-law), and Sholom Calof (her father-in-law) also received assistance.[21]

The surviving records of the JAIAS from the period of Calof family farming are not complete, but Abraham appears periodically in records from the early 1900s. In early 1904, for example, he received a five hundred dollar loan, payable in five annual installments at 6 percent interest.[22] Additional small loans were granted over the next few years, but in 1907 New York denied Abraham's request for two hundred dollars. Perhaps he was too successful at his work by this time, as the grounds for rejection were that "Kalof [sic] could very well get along without further assistance from this Society."[23]

Nineteenth-Century Farm Settlement in North Dakota

Rachel Bella Calof's narrative of homesteading in northeast North Dakota is set in the second settled Jewish rural area of the state. The first major effort began twelve years prior to her 1894 arrival and about two hundred miles to the southwest.[24] Commonly known as Painted Woods after the name of the nearest community, this initial colony stemmed from the vision of Judah Wechsler, a Reform Jewish rabbi in St. Paul who worked tirelessly on various schemes to aid in immigrant settlement and survival.

The Painted Woods Jewish colony began when Wechsler arranged for a land grant on a partially wooded Missouri River tract twenty-five miles north of Bismarck in Burleigh County. The first group of eleven Russian immigrant families settled in the summer of 1882. Hopes for Painted Woods (or "Wechsler's Painted Woods" or even "New Jerusalem," as the settlement was sometimes called) rose during the first year as the colony's numbers increased to over one hundred persons. The high enthusiasm of settlement was unfortunately not balanced with a matching degree of experience in farming or homestead settlement on the part of either the scheme's supporters or the farmers. The first group of settlers arrived too late to plant a crop for 1882 and required continued financial support to survive another twelve months. Some of them also initially located their homes on the school section and thus faced additional legal difficulties in acquiring titles to their homesteads.[25]

From its nascency, the Painted Woods colony was sustained on a lifeline of financial and material contributions. The Hebrew Emigrant Aid Society (HEAS) provided an initial two thousand dollar loan in 1883 and thus began a steady stream of nationwide financial support from individuals, synagogues, and agencies.[26] Wechsler's initial campaign raised over fifteen thousand dollars to make land purchases and to purchase supplies, and his congregation provided food and clothing. Over the next five years, the colonists received over thirty thousand dollars from such diverse sources as HEAS, the Montefiore Agricultural Society (including a short-lived local chapter in Bismarck), and the Hebrew Union Agricultural Society in Cincinnati.

The size of Painted Woods peaked in 1884-85 with over fifty families and 300 individuals, almost all of them Russian and Romanian immigrants. The settlers came to Painted Woods via diverse paths. Some arrived after participation in short-lived rural colonization efforts sponsored by the Baron de Hirsch Fund in Canada, while most others trekked to North Dakota on their own after reading announcements about the colony in the Jewish press.[27] In 1885 the settlers planted 1,400 acres and owned 53 horses, 56 oxen, 61 cows, and 86 calves. They had even established their own school district, whose name of Montefiore has persevered locally almost a century longer than that of any of the original settlement families. The combination of a hard winter in 1884–85, general crop failure in 1885, and drought in 1886 prompted most families to leave and discouraged any new settlers. Their 1886 production record showed 1,800 acres planted and harvests of less than one bushel per acre of wheat. Rabbi Wechsler resigned his St. Paul post in late 1887, and his leave-taking and the final unraveling of the Painted Woods effort occurred in unison.[28]

Devils Lake

By the time of Rachel Bella Calof's arrival in Devils Lake in 1894, Jewish families had resided in rural Ramsey County in northeast North Dakota for more than a decade. Contemporaneous and later accounts of Jewish agrarian settlement efforts in the area typically refer to the entire group as the Devils Lake settlement after the name of the nearest major town.[29] Actually, there were two stages and locations of agrarian activity in the region. The earliest effort centered about six miles east of Garske and about fifteen miles from Devils Lake. The second and much larger community, which included the Calof farms, was about five miles further north and closest to the present town of Starkweather. At the time of settlement, a small village (now defunct) named Iola also existed in the second area. In total, over ninety homestead claims in Ramsey County were made by members of Jewish farm families.[30]

An initial group of twenty-two "Russian Jews" arrived in the Garske area in 1882 through the sponsorship of the Hebrew Emigrant Aid Society.[31] Formal announcements of the settlement soon appeared in the Jewish-American press and information on the community spread to nearby towns via the informal news service of peddlers and other itinerant salesmen.[32] Little is known about the fates of most original members of the Garske group. It appears the settlers suffered through two years of harsh winters and poor crops. Most families disbanded their attempts soon after, leaving behind only the beginning of a cemetery that would continue to serve the rural Jewish population in Ramsey County for another fifty years.

A few of the Garske families joined with some survivors of the Painted Woods colony to form the nucleus of a rural Jewish enclave in the nearby Iola area. Between 1886 and 1894, the number of Jewish farm families increased from around ten to more than forty. The early growth of Jewish rural neighborhoods is in part reflected in the establishment of a post office named Benzion (or, less frequently, Ben Zion) by 1888.[33] The source of this naming is not known. It might well be an expression of the hope (or even the name) of the first postmaster, Benyomen "Benjamin" Greenberg, who envisioned the small settlement as a new Zion in America. Benjamin's father, Abraham Greenberg, had emigrated from the Kiev area to Traverse City, Michigan, where he earned his living peddling in nearby rural areas. After learning about the establishment of Jewish farms near Devils Lake, Abraham and Benjamin visited the area and in 1886 filed on adjacent homesteads.[34] The younger Greenberg became a community leader and was, by all accounts, a colorful local character who preached vegetarianism, led religious services on the holidays, and served as justice of the peace.

The Jewish farming community holdings in 1889 included nearly 3,500 acres of cultivated land, of which 2,650 were in wheat and flax, 300 in oats, and the remainder in barley and potatoes. The increase of the Jewish farm population during the late 1880s largely reflected the availability of credit and philanthropy, the desire of early settlers to reestablish their extended family networks on the Plains, and the diffusion of information on the North Dakota movement to immigrants in midwestern and eastern cities. At least half of the new families arriving in the area were sponsored by settlement loans from New York, Chicago, Minneapolis, or St. Paul. Other newcomers came solely on the advice and call of family members already located in Ramsey County. The reuniting of relatives and friends typically resulted in days of celebration followed by months or even years of additional emotional, physical, and financial pressures. Having exhausted most of their generally meager resources on the move west, new arrivals often spent an extended period living in barns, tents, simple sod structures, or in the already over-crowded one- and two-room houses of earlier settlers. The stability provided by economically viable farming operations was far from the norm. Even those families that managed to fund their own move and an initial year or two on a Ramsey County homestead often turned eventually to philanthropic support for funds to purchase farm machinery, livestock, and building supplies.

Indeed, the ability of many families to survive the first winters or to plant crops each spring seemed to depend on organized emergency relief operations. After a poor crop in 1887, two colony leaders arrived in Minneapolis–St. Paul to ask for help. They received some support from the Sons of Jacob and Mount Zion congregations in St. Paul and from various Minneapolis groups.[35] Similarly, in the winter of 1888-89 residents of Minneapolis and St. Paul sent large shipments of food, clothing, wood, and seeds to the Devils Lake settlers using a free transportation service provided by the St. Paul and Manitoba railroads.

The visits of Jewish farmers to St. Paul also served as a way to recruit new settlers. The first Calofs to arrive in Ramsey County were two of Abraham's cousins, Maier (b. 1868) and Leib (b. 1870) Calof.[36] Their father, Mordechai, had emigrated alone to the United States from the town of Steblev, south of Kiev, in 1884. Although no one is certain how Mordechai Calof became involved in the Painted Woods Colony, this was the destination of his sons and family when they emigrated the following year. The Calofs soon left Burleigh County, however, and for the next two years followed railroad-building employment opportunities from Minnesota to Montana. By 1887 they had relocated in St. Paul. The family next planned a move to Portland, but before leaving Maier met one of the Devils Lake settlers who was in town to request congregational assistance for the farm community. This man "spoke of the settlement in most glorious terms, and pictured the life of the colonists as the most blessed."[37] Perhaps because of Mordechai's miserable experience in Painted Woods, he pleaded with Maier to ignore any impulses to return to the land. But when the rest of his family departed for Portland, Maier took the train to Devils Lake and walked north to find the Jewish farm settlement. About three years later, the family of his Uncle Solomon, with Rachel Bella's future husband Abraham, joined Maier and Leib Calof in Ramsey County.

In the autumn of 1889, Twin Cities residents Jacob Harpman, Joseph Kantrowitz, and E. Rees spent five days in the community and "thoroughly examined everything pertaining to their present standing and future prospects."[38] Their report documented poorly clothed residents, imminent starvation, and few resources to either survive the winter or plant new crops the following spring. They particularly criticized local banks for their high interest rates and for requiring settlers to give annual chattel mortgages on crops and livestock. This latter practice made it possible for creditors to seize the very items that provided farmers with their cash income. In one case cited in the report, a bank reclaimed the livestock and farming implements of a sixty-year-old Jewish man. His creditors feared the settler was about to leave the area "although there was no foundation for such a conclusion." The old man "followed us everywhere, begging for transportation to Chicago, where he might beg a living among his brethen [sic]. He had worn out the clothes and shoes we had furnished him last fall and he was a pitiful sight with tears running down his withered cheeks."[39] The Minneapolis delegation ended their report by recommending the Hebrew Emigrant Aid Society purchase all the chattel mortgages, then totaling between eight and ten thousand dollars.

Contemporaneous reports also reveal various forms of assistance by local agencies and charitable gentile neighbors. The county government, for example, helped organize local relief drives and provided small amounts of food, seed, and other goods. After yet another disastrous harvest in 1890, County Auditor Henry Hale appealed to Judge Myer Isaacs in New York to "investigate conditions [of Jewish families] and see if they are not proper subjects for you to aid." Hale noted the settlers would surely need food and clothing to survive the winter; "fuel," he added, "I believe the County will be able to provide as there is an effort being made to obtain it from the military reservation [Ft. Totten] here."[40]

Most farmers could not keep up with their payments on Jewish agency loans at 6 percent, but at least for a few years their sponsors were likely to extend time payment schedules. Local bank and business debtors held notes at twice the interest rate normally charged by the Jewish organizations. Few creditors of any kind sought foreclosures, perhaps because there were so few assets to claim and most of the homestead land was still under the five-year "proving-up" period and thus still legally owned by the government. Area banks and businesses knew of the Jewish agencies, though, and for a few years at least sought to support the case of their debtors. One month after receiving Hale's letter, the general agent of the JAIAS, A. S. Solomons, received a letter from a Devils Lake businessman by the name of H. C. Hausbrough. Jewish farmers owed him over three thousand dollars for farming implements alone. Hausbrough noted that difficult times "prevail largely among other residents here" and in true agricultural optimism closed by writing that "prospects for a harvest next year are good and if Providence smiles upon the people further assistance will be unnecessary."[41]

Although most financial loans to farmers in North Dakota were tendered on an individual basis, residents occasionally cooperated on a request for their mutual benefit. One of the big problems facing farmers in the Dakotas, for example, was the need to harvest grain crops as soon as they matured. Producers forced to postpone their reaping and thresh-ing faced real risks of crop-devastating frosts, hail, insects, and fires. In 1893, Maier Calof reported that the crop was so

> abundant it took twice as much time to harvest it. A separator [threshing machine] was needed; not one was available in the colony. It took me a few days before I returned with the machine and the day I came back was the eve of Rosh Hashanah, the Jewish New Year. We had to postpone the work until after the holidays. There is an old Yiddish saying: "The man thinks and God laughs."[42] And we, too, felt God's laughter, for on the second day of Rosh Hashanah,[43] a heavy rain occurred and later a white snow fell. It was a great blow to all of us. The difficulties were partly overcome, but with hard labor and heavy losses to the crop. The stacks of grain froze and this later molded. The commodity had to be sold for a lesser price which did not even cover our expenses in the end."[44]

A group of Ramsey County farmers approached both JAAS and JAIAS for money to purchase a steam engine and grain separator. After four years of documenting the need for the machinery, the New York society

A minyan on the Calof farm, circa 1910.

granted a loan of $2,182 at 6 percent interest. In the first year of work, the settlers used the machinery to thresh over 16,500 bushels of grain, including over 8,500 bushels of flax, their principal cash crop. One of the beneficiaries of the machinery, Philip Greenberg, told Abraham Levy of the JAAS that this "is the first time that the crop of the Jewish farmers had been threshed before November since they have been here."[45]

Greater economic stability existed in the Jewish farm community from around 1898 to 1907, although the overall population number decreased during that time from approximately thirty to twenty families.[46] Families continued to move in and out of the area, but the pace of exchange seems no more dramatic than in most other North Dakota areas during the same period. The core of the Jewish community solidified in a region encompassing the southern sections of Overland and Sullivan Townships and northern portions of Cato and Harding Townships.[47] Plat maps of Jewish family locations show that their farmsteads were typically intermingled with those of other immigrant groups, particularly Norwegians and German-Russians. In the case of the Calofs, however, members of the family were able to file on adjoining tracts forming a one-mile-square holding. Each family eventually built their homes, barns, and granaries near the common center corner. According to one recent oral history, this enclave is still referred to as "Little Jerusalem" in local place naming.[48]

Rachel Bella Calof's narrative portrays an unmistakably Jewish home-steading experience, though she does not provide details on the institutional organization of Judaism in the Devils Lake area. There was no regular rabbi in the region from the time of first settlement until the early 1890s. Special or formal needs were satisfied by the visits of rabbis, shochets, and mohels[49] from St. Paul, Minneapolis, Grand Forks, or other larger towns. One figure who stands out in collective memory of early itinerant religious visitors was Sam Yaffee, the shamus of the Sons of Abraham Synagogue in St. Paul.[50] Although most of Yaffee's visits lasted only one or two days, on several occasions he stayed for a few weeks to take care of the training and preparations for a boy's bar mitzvah.

During these years many High Holiday services were held in the home of Philip Greenberg, who not only had one of the largest homes in the area but also reportedly owned a Torah given to his family by Moses Montefiore.[51] As the Devils Lake community grew in size and additional families settled in area towns, High Holiday services were held in the courtroom in the county building in Devils Lake. According to a former resident, "all judicial business was suspended" on Rosh Hashanah and Yom Kippur.[52]

Beginning in 1892, Rabbi Benjamin Papermaster from Grand Forks served the settlement as religious leader, mohel, and shochet. For a few years, his appearances in the rural farming area was "on demand and availability" as families called on his services for bar mitzvahs, weddings, or funerals. Rabbi Papermaster began to make more regular visits in the late 1890s as the community began to show signs of permanence in both numbers and fiscal resources.[53] He scheduled special spring and fall visits to prepare kosher meat, although some residents continued to have frozen kosher meat shipped to them from Grand Forks during winter months. Rabbi Papermaster's son recalled one summer visit in which the Calofs are mentioned:

> My father took me along on one of his trips there. . . . We were met at Devils Lake station by one of the Caloffs [sic] with an ox-cart; that is, an ox hitched to a two wheeled sulky. There was not enough room for me on the sulky seat so I sat in front. The ox switched more flies off me than he did off himself. One can only imagine a 30 mile ride over a country road by ox power.[54]

There were probably no more than ten Jewish families farming in Ramsey County when Rachel Bella and Abraham Calof left their farm in 1917. Vestiges of the colony persisted for another decade, and the last of the older settlement families left the land in the mid-1920s. Some families migrated to Devils Lake or nearby towns; others, like the Calofs, opted to relocate initially in the Twin Cities area, and a few followed the railroad or movement of homesteading opportunities to the North-west.[55]

Almost all of the sacred and secular transformations of the landscape made by the Jewish farm families in the region are now gone. Some of these, like the rough *mikvah*[56] the settlers formed by widening and boarding a small portion of an open prairie slough, would hardly be comprehensible to local residents. In addition to occasional place names grounded in a chapter of local history now unknown to most North Dakotans, the single tangible reminder of a Jewish presence is the "Sons of Jacob" cemetery located about three miles east of Starkweather and six miles northeast of Garske. Established by the first Garske group in 1885 on unsurveyed land, the graveyard ended up officially located on a tract transferred from federal to state ownership and then sold to a non-Jewish resident in 1902. At least twenty-seven Jewish families responded by petitioning the governor to allow their purchase of a small parcel, including the cemetery. The signers named themselves as "The Russian Hebrew Church Society" and included most of the Calof males.[57]

The Fate of Jewish Farmers in the Heartland

By 1965 only three of close to 46,500 rural households surveyed in North Dakota had any Jewish ancestry at all. Similar reports in recent decades of the ethnicity of farm families in other midwestern states all seem to deny the existence of any earlier movement of Jewish families onto Heartland farms. We are more sure of the short-term fate of the settlers than of the reasons why their experiences ended as they did. Although exact percentages of particular lengths of farm tenure cannot be stated, certainly the majority of families did not stay on their original farms for more than seven years. While some tried farming again in a new area, more typically the agricultural experiment ended in a move into a town either in the region or to the west. Further, the experience of Rachel Bella Calof typifies that of families who eventually established viable farming operations and even became relatively prosperous and successful. Only infrequently, perhaps in less than 2 percent of all attempts, did a farm continue in operation with a second generation.

With no continuous Jewish farming presence two generations re-moved from initial settlement, it may be supposed that the farm move-ment was a general failure. Such an assessment would be accurate from some perspectives. Certainly farming never provided many settlers with any long-term economic panacea. And the cost of the experiment was especially high for families in which parents lost children because of a lack of rudimentary medical attention or children lost a parent in a prairie blizzard. To historians blinkered by statistics on farm longevity and tenure, the Jewish farm experience makes a rather miserable show-ing against other ethnic groups in the Midwest (even though most of them had higher rates of occupational mobility and farm loss than is usually assumed). A host of practical reasons can readily explain what appear to be the failures of Jewish farm settlement, including lack of agricultural experience, generally poor choices of land at a time preced-ing the development of effective local farming systems, and low capital

resources apart from the sustenance provided by charities and philanthropies.

It is evident, however, that Jewish families left farming under at least
two basic circumstances: those who were unable to survive for very long
needed to pursue other opportunities, and those who were able to
survive deliberately renounced continued farm life to pursue other
opportunities. The latter group includes most of the extended Calof clan
and also many settlers who "proved out" their homesteads, acquired
title, and then sold their land for a stake large enough to enter other lines
of work in towns and cities. Farming for these individuals, who had
experienced years of hardship and low prices, served in part as a step up
an economic ladder. Farming, even if it provided a living, could be
rejected for reasons beyond those that had prompted the initial settlement. Once the original impulses (e.g., owning land, being your own
boss) were satisfied, there remained other desirable ends to pursue.

Rachel Bella Calof's narrative reveals that the problems and shortcom-
ings of homesteading were not confined to the pragmatics of farm life
and economic needs. As is characteristic of the farm diaries and reminiscences from other ethnic immigrant groups, the loneliness of the
homestead and the solitary existence of rural areas in the Midwest
contrasted sharply with the more communal nature of urban and rural
life throughout much of the Old World. Adding poverty to isolation
exacerbated feelings of being cut off physically and socially from the rest
of one's social identity. Tasks repeated daily or chores requiring endless
repetition occupied the days and exhausted the body, but the mind and
spirit remained unfulfilled. The son of a Michigan farmer recalls his
father telling of

> waking up at three in the morning because he could hear his grandmother
> scolding his grandfather. It was not that she believed him to be at fault with
> regard to any particular matter; she was simply so bored that she would start an
> argument to add some spice to her life. As my father said, "What on earth could
> you argue about in Bad Axe [Michigan] at three in the morning?" Nothing
> changed; it was a constant sameness of the struggle; we didn't even get a daily
> newspaper.[58]

Beyond the short-term requirements of daily survival, farm families of all ethnic and religious heritages also had to cope with the long-term pressures and implications of central cultural values and group continuity. Jewish Heartland farmers did not stay long enough on their farms to develop common distinctive cultural practices regarding agricultural production or farming worldviews. Their decisions to leave the land, and especially the lack of intergenerational continuity after short-term successes, reveal aspects of core cultural values and attitude systems brought to the farm. Two obvious manifestations of this pattern were emphases on education and endogamous marriage. In combination with the relative isolation from both other Jewish families and educational institutions, norms of marriage and education drove children away from the farm rather than supporting continuity. The internationally arranged marriage of Rachel Bella Calof sufficed for some of the Old World-born who had connections to their former homes and who ascribed to customs permitting such matchmaking by professional *shadchen*.[59] To their American-born children, the practice was not only less practical but also far less culturally acceptable.

Grown children finding spouses outside the farm community and pursuing opportunities for higher education in larger towns and cities tended to settle in these other areas to raise their families and to pursue careers commensurate with their education. And although some Jewish children went to land-grant universities or pursued agriculture-related degrees, this was not an era when college educations were necessary or normal components of farm training. And so, as the children left the farm, their parents eventually followed them.

It is difficult to conceive of the continued presence of successful Jewish farmers without the parallel development of successful Jewish rural communities. The key here is that the potential preservation of "Jewishness" (or "Norwegianness" or "Catholicness") depends in part on the ability of a group of people to maintain a particular cultural distinctiveness. Isolated individuals might be able to sustain their cultural heritage over a long period of time, but transgenerational continuity would seem highly unlikely, if not impossible, without a social context in which to effect and collectively support the maintenance of this heritage. Jewish farm families generally did not have access to either the formal cultural contexts or social support networks required to develop a stable community. They worried particularly about the dilution of their heritage and the strength of their *yiddishkeit* ("Jewishness") and the impact of *goyishkeit* ("gentileness"). Philip Cowen, editor of the *American Hebrew*, noted that "of all their complaints, in spite of all their hardships, the religious education of the young seemed to concern [the farmers] the most."[60] This worry was not reflected in immediate anxieties about particular religious or ethnic expressions as much as in a more widespread concern to perpetuate a larger heritage and a cultural value system.

The immigrant experience on the plains thus involved both internal and external struggles. In spirit similar to Ole Edvart Rölvaag's trilogy on Norwegian experiences on the northern plains,[61] Rachel Bella Calof's story reveals the stresses occurring within families, between families, and in the relations of the immigrant group to the dominant society. We are greatly indebted to her for having the honesty, motivation, and skill to share these complex issues with us.

Notes

1. This research was supported by fellowships from the American Jewish Archives (Cincinnati Campus, Hebrew Union College) and the National Endowment for the Humanities. Special appreciation is extended to Abe Peck, Jacob Marcus, and Fannie Zelcher for their assistance and guidance during research visits in Cincinnati.

2. The most comprehensive treatment of the formalized Heartland communal efforts is Uri Herscher, *Jewish Agricultural Utopias in America, 1880–1910* (Detroit: Wayne State University Press, 1981).

3. Violet Goering and Orlando J. Goering, "Jewish Farmers in South Dakota—The *Am Olam*," *South Dakota History* 12:4 (1982): 232–47, and "The Agricultural Communes of the *Am Olam*," *Communal Societies* 16 (1985): 74–86.

4. Cohen's account of the experiment is *In Quest of Heaven* (New York: Sunrise History Publishing Committee, 1957).

5. The total for the Heartland states is about 19 percent of the estimated total Jewish farm population in the country; see Leonard G. Robinson, *The Agricultural Activities of the Jews in America* (New York: American Jewish Committee, 1912), pp. 58–59.

6. The Pale of Settlement refers to a region of western Russia designated in 1791 as the area in which all Jews had to reside. Stretching from Baltic Sea to Black Sea, it included Ukraine, Byelorussia, Lithuania, and much of Poland (granted to Russia in 1772).

7. Richard E. Singer, "The American Jew in Agriculture: Past History and Present Condition," unpublished essay, 1941, American Jewish Archives, Cincinnati Campus, Hebrew Union College, Jewish Institute of Religion; and Leo Shpall, "Jewish Agricultural Colonies in the United States," *Agricultural History* 24 (1950): 120–46.

8. One exception to this pattern was a short-lived collaboration in the summer and fall of 1891 between Jacob H. Schiff of New York, representing the Baron de Hirsch Fund, and James Hill, the head of the Great Northern Railway Company. They eventually agreed on a plan to develop a large tract of railroad land near Millaca, Minnesota. Although the Fund contributed some financial backing and Hill organized the building of tract housing for prospective settlers, no more than a few families ever moved onto the land. See Cyrus Adler, *Jacob H. Schiff: His Life and Letters*, vol. 2 (Garden City, N.Y.: Doubleday, Doran, 1928), pp. 87–88; James J. Hill Correspondence, Minnesota Historical Society, St. Paul; and James J. Hill Papers, Hill Reference Library, St. Paul.

9. Examples regarding North Dakota include Henry Kremens, self-recorded taped reminiscences, 1974, Upper Midwest Jewish Historical Society, St. Paul; and Charles Losk, "Journal," unpublished manuscript, American Jewish Archives, Cincinnati Campus, Hebrew Union College. Also see Joel S. Geffen, "Jewish Agricultural Colonies as Reported in the Pages of the Russian Hebrew Press *Ha-Meliz* and *Ha-Yom*," *American Jewish History Quarterly* 60:4 (1971): 355–82.

10. Abraham R. Levy, "The Promotion of Husbandry among the Jewish Poor," *American Israelite* 47:50 (June 13, 1901), p. 1.

11. The word "colony" is used here to designate any settlement of multiple Jewish families within a contiguous rural area. The word should not imply any particular structure of landownership, sponsorship, or political boundaries.

12. *The Jewish Agriculturalists' Aid Society of America Report for the Year 1903* (Chicago: n.p., 1904), p. ii.

13. *The Jewish Agriculturalists' Aid Society of America Report for the Year 1901* (Chicago: n.p., 1902), p. 5.

14. J. Sanford Rikoon, "Ethnicity, Philanthropy, and Agriculture in the Heartland: The Case of the Jewish Agriculturalists' Aid Society of America" (paper presented at the American Jewish Historical Society National Conference, Omaha, Neb., May 1990).

15. Levy, "The Promotion of Husbandry," p. 1. Emphasis in the original.

16. Perhaps de Hirsch's most famous plan was an offer of fifty million francs (or roughly $10 million at the time) to the Russian Czar to improve conditions, particularly educational opportunities, in Jewish areas. De Hirsch withdrew his proposal after almost a year of fruitless negotiation in 1887–88.

17. Although written as a testimonial publication, the most comprehensive treatment of the fund's first forty years is Samuel Joseph, *History of the Baron de Hirsch Fund* (New York: Jewish Publication Society, 1935).

18. Baron de Hirsch, "Refuge for Russian Jews," *The Forum* 11 (August 1891): 627; quoted in Joseph, *Baron de Hirsch Fund*, p. 12.

19. Arthur Reichow, "Memoir of the Work of the Year 1898," unpublished report of the Agriculture and Industry Department of the Baron de Hirsch Fund, January 12,

1899, p. 1, Archive Collections of the American Jewish Historical Society, Waltham, Mass.

20. In 1922, JAIAS formally changed its name to the Jewish Agricultural Society. For a comprehensive description of the agency and its activities, see Gabriel Davidson, *Our Jewish Farmers* (New York: L. B. Fischer, 1943).

21. *The Jewish Agriculturalists' Aid Society of America Report for the Year 1908* (Chicago: n.p., 1909), p. 65. Regretfully, the annual reports provide only the name and year of loans to farmers and the number of adults and children in each family. The unpublished records of the society's loans and almost all other business records appear no longer to exist.

22. The entry for this loan notes the farm subject only to one prior debt of $900. One of Abraham's brothers, Savol Calof, received a similar JAIAS loan that year as well. Minutes, the Jewish Agricultural and Industrial Aid Society, March 2, 1904, p. 425, Archive Collections of the American Jewish Historical Society, Waltham, Mass.

23. Minutes, the Jewish Agricultural and Industrial Aid Society, October 30, 1907, Archive Collections of the American Jewish Historical Society, Waltham, Mass.

24. On their own, individual Jewish immigrants attempted to farm in North Dakota prior to the 1880s, particularly in the Red River Valley. One account of such an attempt is Henry and Lea Fine, "North Dakota Memories," *Western States Jewish Historical Quarterly* 9:4 (1977): 331–40.

25. William C. Sherman, "Jewish Homestead Communities in North Dakota, 1880–1920" (paper presented at the Seventeenth Annual Northern Great Plains History Conference, Bemidji, Minn., Oct. 1982), p. 6, and correspondence of Rose Lenitsky to W. Gunther Plaut, March 1958, Archive Collections of the American Jewish Historical Society, Waltham, Mass.

26. The Painted Woods effort coincided with the even more highly publicized colonization attempt of Beersheba in southwest Kansas. Cincinnati's Rabbi Isaac Mayer Wise conceived and championed this effort and was instrumental in organizing the Hebrew Union Agricultural Society in Cincinnati to spearhead the colony's development. For a rather detailed chronicle of the earliest portions of the Beersheba Colony experience, see Charles K. Davis, "Diary," unpublished manuscript in the American Jewish Archives, Cincinnati Campus, Hebrew Union College. Portions of this diary are reprinted in *American Jewish Archives* 17:2 (1965): 119–34. Also see A. James Rudin, "Beersheba, Kansas: 'God's Pure Air on Government Land,'" *Kansas Historical Quarterly* 34:3 (1968): 282–98, and Lipman G. Feld, "New Light on the Lost Jewish Colony at Beersheba, Kansas," *American Jewish Historical Quarterly* 40:1 (1970): 159–68.

27. At least one group of settlers came directly from Odessa following the pogroms there in 1881 and 1882. See Eugene Nudelman, "The Family of Joseph Nudelman," unpublished family memoir [1969], American Jewish Archives, Cincinnati Campus, Hebrew Union College, and Dorothy Dellar Kohanski, "The Saga of Solomon Dellar and His Children," unpublished manuscript, copy in author's private possession.

28. For more on Painted Woods, see W. Gunther Plaut, *The Jews in Minnesota: The First Seventy-five Years* (New York: American Jewish Historical Society, 1959), pp. 96–103, and Lois Fields Schwartz, "Early Jewish Agricultural Colonies in North Dakota," *North Dakota History* 32:4 (1965): 217–32.

29. Other accounts refer to the Jewish rural communities as the Garske, Starkweather, Iola, and Chananel settlements.

30. William C. Sherman, *Prairie Mosaic: An Ethnic Atlas of Rural North Dakota* (Fargo: North Dakota Institute for Regional Studies, 1983), p. 112.

31. Plaut, *Jews in Minnesota*, p. 105, quoting an unsubstantiated report in the Bismarck newspaper, December 1882.

32. Interview with Dr. and Mrs. Irwin Epstein, interviewer and date unknown, the Leo M. Franklin Archives, Temple Beth El, Birmingham, Mich. Mrs. Epstein was the daughter of Philip Greenberg, who settled in the Garske area in 1884. Also see James E. Myers, questionnaire return in unpublished and undated survey conducted by the Jewish Agricultural Society, Archive Collections of the American Jewish Historical Society, Waltham, Mass.

33. The earliest known reference to the "Benzion" post office is in the 1888 loan records of the Jewish Agriculturalists' Aid Society. The post office closed in 1902 and the nearest service was then in Garske. Interestingly, a list of post offices in North Dakota at the time of statehood (1889) lists a "Jerusalem" post office in Ramsey County. No references to this name have been located in any writings on or by resident Jewish farm families.

34. Correspondence of Nettie Greenberg Epstein to the Jewish Historical Society of Michigan, January 10, 1979, the Leo M. Franklin Archives, Temple Beth El, Birmingham, Mich. Benjamin's brother, Philip, filed for a homestead one year later.

35. Discussions over support of the Devils Lake community appear to have created quite a bit of controversy between St. Paul and Minneapolis congregations. Although this struggle was likely symptomatic of deeper issues having little to do with questions of philanthropy, the groups managed to carry their heated battles onto the pages of the *American Israelite*. See Plaut, *Jews in Minnesota*, pp. 105–108.

36. Maier Calof claimed land in Section 33 and Leib in Section 29 of Township 157 North, Range 63 West, in Sullivan Township.

37. Maier Calof, *Miracles of the Lives of Maier and Doba Calof* (privately printed, 1941). Maier Calof compiled his reminiscence at the age of seventy-three.

38. Correspondence of J. Harpman, R. Rees, J. Kantrowitz, J. Skoll, and E. Bernstein to M. Isaacs, I. Strauss, and D. Goldman, September 17, 1889, Archive Collections of the American Jewish Historical Society, Waltham, Mass.

39. Ibid. Such experiences were not confined to Jewish immigrants in Ramsey County. The report told of a Norwegian settler who "drove a spike into his head with a mallet" after losing everything to a creditor charging "exhorbitant [sic] interest."

40. Correspondence of Henry Hale to Judge M. I. Isaacs, October 17, 1890, Archive Collections of the American Jewish Historical Society, Waltham, Mass.

41. Correspondence of H. C. Hausbrough to A. S. Solomons, November 18, 1890, Archive Collections of the American Jewish Historical Society, Waltham, Mass.

42. This is a literal translation of the Yiddish proverb "der mentsh tracht, un Got lacht." A more well-known variant of this saying is "Man proposes, God disposes."

43. Throughout most of the Jewish diaspora, Rosh Hashanah is celebrated for two days. These days mark the beginning of a ten-day period of repentance (*Aseret Y'mei T'shuva*) ending with the holiday of Yom Kippur.

44. Calof, *Miracles in the Lives of Maier and Doba Calof*, p. 29.

45. *JAAS Report for 1901*, p. 14.

46. This period of relative stability was aided by generally favorable crop-growing conditions, an upturn in market prices after 1895, and the completion of a railroad connection to Garske in 1902.

47. Sherman, "Jewish Homestead Communities," p. 8.

48. Sherman, "Jewish Homestead Communities," p. 16, and Robert J. Lazar, "From Ethnic Minority to Socio-economic Elite: A Study of the Jewish Community of Fargo, North Dakota" (Ph.D. diss., University of Minnesota, 1958), p. 55.

49. *Shochets* are ritual slaughterers authorized to prepare and evaluate meats according to the rules of the *kashrut* (dietary laws). *Mohels* are technicians able to perform ritual circumcision of male babies.

50. Correspondence of Nettie Greenberg Epstein to Jewish Historical Society of Michigan, January 10, 1979, Archive Collections of the American Jewish Historical Society, Waltham, Mass. The role of the *shamus* is difficult to describe and is perhaps closest to that of a sexton. The *shamus* performed many organizational duties for both the congregation and religious hierarchy, but often had a greater leadership and teaching role in small congregations.

51. The provenance of the Torah possessed by the Greenbergs is outlined in a family narrative related by Nettie Greenberg Epstein in 1979. According to this story, the Greenbergs were related to Sir Moses Montefiore (1784–1885). At the time of Montefiore's one-hundredth birthday, the Greenbergs were living in Traverse City, Michigan, and the small group of Jews there had no Torah. Nettie's grandfather, Abraham, wrote to Montefiore and told him of their plight. In turn the leader of England's Jewish community sent Abraham the Torah he brought to North Dakota in 1887. This Torah reportedly remained in Ramsey County until 1907, when one of Abraham Greenberg's sons took it to St. Paul (correspondence of Nettie Greenberg Epstein, January 10, 1979, Archive Collections of the American Jewish Historical Society, Waltham, Mass.).

The story of this Torah's acquisition is interesting also because it is part of a larger corpus of legends attached to the largesse of Sir Montefiore. Gunther Plaut (*Jews in Minnesota*, p. 103), for example, claims that Rabbi Wechsler of St. Paul "wrote all the way to England's Sir Moses Montefiore to obtain a *sefer torah* for the colony" at Painted Woods.

52. Correspondence from Sheldon Karlins to Jacob Marcus, December 3, 1982, American Jewish Archives, Cincinnati Campus, Hebrew Union College.

53. For more on Rabbi Benjamin Papermaster's life in North Dakota, see the three-part series by Isadore Papermaster, "A History of North Dakota Jewry and Their Pioneer Rabbi," *Western States Jewish Historical Quarterly* 10:1 (1978): 74–89; 10:2 (1978): 170–84; and 10:3 (1978): 266–93.

54. "Memoirs" of Isadore Papermaster, unpublished manuscript, p. 22, Special Collections, Chester Fritz Library, North Dakota State University, Fargo.

55. Other Jewish settlements occurred in North Dakota after the start of the Devils Lake colony. Almost all of them started around 1900, reached their peak numbers in the early 1910s, and declined rapidly after World War I. The largest group farmed in McIntosh County near the towns of Ashley and Wishek. Sometimes called the Sulzberger Colony, after the famed New York philanthropist, the colony eventually included more than sixty families. A slightly smaller number of families settled near the communities of Wing and Regan in present-day McLean County. Although located in the general proximity of the old Painted Woods colony, the later effort persevered longer in part due to the availability of off-farm labor in the Wilton coal-mining region. The last area to be settled that eventually grew to include at least forty families was in Bowman

County. Finally, mention should be made of smaller groups of ten to twenty families who resided for short periods in Bottineau County and Morton County.

56. The *mikvah* is the ritual bath prescribed for women at the end of their menstrual period or following the birth of a child. The Devils Lake *mikvah* is noted in Calof, *Miracles of the Lives of Maier and Doba Calof*, p. 25.

57. Correspondence from "The Russian Hebrew Church Society of Ramsey County, North Dakota" to [North Dakota Governor] Frank White, December 23, 1903, Collections of the American Jewish Archives, Cincinnati Campus, Hebrew Union College. The petitioners were eventually successful in their request. In the fall of 1903 they purchased five acres for $62.53 (correspondence of [Ramsey County Auditor] Emil Eich to Philip Greenberg, August 24, 1903, Collections of the American Jewish Archives).

58. Correspondence of Stanley J. Ellias to Irving I. Katz, March 29, 1977, the Leo M. Franklin Archives, Temple Beth El, Birmingham, Mich.

59. Interestingly, Abraham Calof's two cousins in the Benzion area, Maier and Leib Calof, married sisters (Doba and Sarah Zaslavsky) who came to North Dakota only after an arranged marriage orchestrated by an uncle in Steblev. See Calof, *Miracles of the Lives of Maier and Doba Calof*, pp. 22–26.

60. Philip Cowen, commentary on letter from Bennie Greenberg (Ramsey County, N.D.), *The American Hebrew*, January 25, 1901, pp. 317–18.

61. Ole Edvart Rölvaag's trilogy was first published in English as *Giants in the Earth: A Saga of the Prairie*, trans. Lincoln Colcord and the author (New York: Harper & Brothers, 1927); *Peder Victorious: A Tale of the Pioneers Twenty Years Later*, trans. Nora O. Solum and the author (New York: Harper & Brothers, 1929); and *Their Father's God*, trans. Trygve M. Ager (New York: Harper & Brothers, 1931).

RACHEL BELLA CALOF'S LIFE AS COLLECTIVE HISTORY

Elizabeth Jameson

University of New Mexico

Rachel Bella Calof needs, in the most basic sense, no elaboration. She speaks so clearly for herself that it has often felt like unnecessary hubris to try to add to her words. The broader contexts of her life, however, help us read her autobiography as a historical document and see her acts as history. Rachel Bella Calof writes from the interior spaces of private life, and, from that vantage point, reconfigures more familiar versions of the American West. The result is simultaneously a historical record, and, insistently and candidly, the life of a particular woman with an individual voice. Respect for the woman and for the honesty of her self-revelation urges reciprocal clarity in how we read her life.

Rachel Bella Kahn Calof came to me as an unexpected gift from Sandy Rikoon, who recognized the broad significance of her narrative, and from Jacob Calof, who made his mother's story accessible to a wider audience. Asked to provide interpretive contexts for her memoir, I opened it at eleven o'clock one night, intending a quick skim after a long evening grading exams. I didn't get to bed until almost four the next morning.

Rachel Bella Calof's story hooked me from several directions at once. I read her as a historian, drawn by an unromantic account of a woman homesteader; as a woman far removed from the homestead frontier, juggling family, household, and personal space; and as a Jew whose great-grandfather, like the Calofs, left Russia and emigrated to the United States in the late nineteenth century. Each level of engagement seemed to demand a different response.

Locating Rachel Bella Calof in historical context is not a simple matter of putting her in a particular place and time, much as we might slide a missing piece into a jigsaw puzzle of an old frontier landscape. She doesn't fit the West of popular history or collective imagination. Nor, for that matter, does she slip easily into familiar pictures of Jewish immigrants, or of the women of turn-of-the-century America. Women, immigrants, and the West evoke a series of unconnected images.

The West of popular imagination is a panorama of wide, rolling spaces, punctuated with cowboys, lawmen, fur trappers, prospectors, soldiers, or ranchers, surrounded by buffalo, antelope, and longhorn cattle. If we see an occasional woman, she is either a brief distraction in a saloon or brothel, or else a hazy figure, far in the background, angelically supportive or stoically resigned, a prop for some rugged man who struggles to wrest a better future from a difficult land.[1]

Shifting our focus to Jewish immigrants, we might imagine huddled refugees at Ellis Island, wan and hopeful, grateful to emerge from endless days in steerage. Their arduous journeys carry them from oppressive pasts to uncertain but promising futures. They start their search for better lives virtually where they disembark. These Jews remain in the East, moving no farther than a nearby urban ghetto. Their bustling historic backdrop is teeming streets, pushcarts, synagogues, crowded tenements, and grimy sweatshops where women sew ceaselessly for a meager wage.[2]

Turning our gaze to "more prominent" women, we might imagine

Victorian ladies corseted into hourglass figures and genteel, suffering passivity. These women barely move at all. Too fragile for action, too refined for men's ambitions or animal lusts, they ornament elaborately contrived parlors, havens from the tainted world of commercial competition. Sheltered and encased in domestic cocoons, their dependency mutely demonstrates the worldly status of male providers.[3]

It is hard to imagine genteel women or immigrant Jews next to cowboys and covered wagons. These combinations seem incongruous because they juxtapose distorted and partial images, the caricatures and stereotypes of popular myths and dated history. Popular conventions do not prepare us to find Rachel Bella Calof on a homestead in Ramsey County, North Dakota. If she does not belong, then we can read her as an extraordinary but unrepresentative woman, interesting on her own terms, but not beyond. To see her fully, in our collective story, we must probe the historical assumptions she violates. We must abandon the imagined West that excludes her.

Our historical visions of a masculine Euro-American West developed largely from Frederick Jackson Turner's frontier thesis, which located such key American traits as individualism and democracy in white men's encounters with a number of successive frontiers. Turner wrote over a century ago, and historians have debated and revised him ever since.[4] More recent works by new western historians emphasize diversities of race, ethnicity, class, and gender; conflicts among groups; contested claims to resources; social adaptation and cultural change; and relationships of power and dependency. The land itself, once portrayed as empty and virginal, becomes already inhabited and always changing, as natural processes and human use reconfigure both cultures and the land.[5]

One new area of exploration is the subfield of western women's history. Convinced that accurate western history required a complete cast of characters, historians worked to document western women's experiences and then to write new histories with women as subjects of their own lives, rather than as supporting figures in other peoples' stories.[6] It was hard at first to envision how an inclusive history would change inherited versions of the past. The first histories of western women placed them in borrowed plots and conceptual frameworks, starting with the nineteenth-century frontiers of Turnerian history and their liberating influence for Americans. Did the West offer women greater democracy and economic opportunity? Did the frontier enable women to escape the limited roles prescribed for women of the Victorian middle class? These concerns reflected older western histories and more recent histories of eastern women. The more optimistic argued that the West liberated women because women first voted in western states and territories, and because the Homestead Act of 1862 allowed unmarried women to file for land in their own names. Less sanguine interpretations suggested that neither votes nor property ended women's private subordination, that women often moved West against their own wishes, and that they were frequently isolated, abused, and oppressed by constant childbearing and physical labor.[7]

Western women's historians soon rejected the narrow focus on Euro-American frontierswomen and the limited questions of older histories, calling instead for an expanded time frame, for multicultural inclusiveness, and for reconceiving history from women's own perspectives.[8] New histories examined women's adaptations to western environments, their roles in cross-cultural encounters, their efforts to establish social networks and community institutions, and changing understandings of gender—the behaviors, values, and meanings attached to the biological fact of being male or female.

Gender is a plastic historical category, distinct from sex. Histories that excluded women assumed that women's lives were determined by biology and were thus unchanging and ahistorical. New histories of women and gender explored how different people rearranged their personal relationships, family and kinship, work, childbearing and childrearing, and men's and women's public and private power. One of the most important tasks, and for many of us the most difficult, was imagining a history that did not center on native-born Euro-Americans.

The desire for more accurate and inclusive histories led us to seek new sources that recorded the experiences of "ordinary" people in all their variety.⁹ That is why Rachel Bella Calof's memoir is so engrossing. The most basic sites of human experience are often the hardest to document. Yet the intimate arenas of households and families are where most of us learn the values, roles, and expectations that influence our social behavior. Private experience informs public action. Social isolation and parental concern often motivated settlers to establish schools, synagogues, and libraries and to sponsor the celebrations that knit communities in the West. The intimate details of settlement help us understand larger processes that intrigue historians—how institutions were re-created and transformed in the West, how various immigrants adapted culturally to new environments, and, for women's historians, how gender relations changed as men and women stretched the behaviors and options considered appropriate for each sex.

Through the intimate details of her pioneer life, Rachel Bella Calof jars the standard formulas and the recognized story lines of older frontier histories. Her westward journey began in Russia, not on a worn-out eastern farm. She traveled by sea and rail, not covered wagon. She sought opportunities defined not by the infinite promise of a new land, but by the limited options of the old. For her, the wide western spaces did not signify boundless promise but served rather as places of occasional privacy and escape from new family obligations that engulfed and stifled her. The prairie provided refuge as well from an interior domestic world she often found cramped, crowded, and constricted. She did not achieve the happy ending of fictional pioneers, who lived securely ever after on their hard-won land. And, of course, she was not a native-born pioneer, but an immigrant, a woman, a Jew.

Rachel Bella Calof violates the cozy nostalgia of pioneer families cheerfully persevering on "Little House on the Prairie" homesteads. The seductive image they evoke of perpetual warmth, support, and cooperation establishes a difficult standard for real families forced to mediate daily stresses, competing needs, and interpersonal accommodations. In contrast, Rachel Bella Calof tells, with matter-of-fact realism, a story that is both unique and a representative western tale. Rachel Bella Calof was not, in any simple sense, a "typical" western pioneer. But neither, in a more complex sense, was she wildly unusual.

The sheer demography of the West bears this out. Euro-American pioneers encountered a West that was the most ethnically diverse section of the United States. From 1860 to 1900, between a fourth and a third of the western population was foreign born, proportionately more than in any other census region.[10] "Westerners" were an enormously diverse lot. Their heritage includes the histories of American Indian cultures, the Spanish-Mexican frontier, Chinese and Japanese laborers, French trappers and fur traders, African American cowboys and cavalry soldiers, and an enormous variety of European immigrants. Most of these westerners, including most women, were marginal at best in traditional frontier histories.

Although western men outnumbered women on many frontiers, and well into the twentieth century, the real West was never as unremittingly masculine as the imagined West.[11] Some Indian women married European men; together they engendered new metis and mestizo cultures.[12] European and Euro-American women often came West later than men. They were generally outnumbered on the fur trade frontier, in mining camps, in military garrisons, and on ranches. Family settlement was most common in agricultural areas, and the proportion of men to women there least unequal.

The Calofs' North Dakota attracted an ethnically diverse farm population, largely families or single men, with a significant minority of independent women homesteaders. In 1890, four years before Rachel Bella Calof first glimpsed the Devils Lake railroad station, North Dakota's population was 44 percent female, and about equally foreign born. The immigrants included large numbers of Norwegians, Germans from Russia, Canadians, Germans, and Swedes. Most of the native born were the children of immigrants, and only one North Dakotan in five was a native-born child of native-born parents.[13]

Ramsey County, where the Calofs settled, mirrored the state. Its population in 1880 was 33.5 percent immigrant; ten years later, it was almost 42 percent. The Calofs joined an influx of settlers who swelled the county population from 281 in 1880 to over 15,000 by 1920.[14] Part of that increase came from reproduction. Rachel Bella Calof spoke for many women when she wryly declared that "personally the most dependable state of affairs I knew during the many years I lived on the prairie was pregnancy." Native-born newcomers and immigrants' children shrank the proportion of the population that was foreign-born to 31 percent in 1900. Statewide, 24,000 second-generation North Dakotans claimed Russian ancestry, including large numbers of Germans from Russia as well as the smaller communities of Russian Jews.[15]

Ramsey County place names reflected the diverse origins of its settlers. Besides the Benzion post office, the census listed Norway, Odessa, Ontario, Sullivan, South Minnewaukan, De Groat, and Lillehof townships.[16] People of Russian ancestry were the third-largest immigrant group, outnumbered only by the Canadians and Norwegians. The people of Ramsey County, who came from at least twenty-two foreign countries, included Danes, Swedes, Germans, Czechs, Poles, Finns, Hungarians, and Greeks. During the Calofs' homesteading years, the local demography changed only slightly, to include more children of immigrants in the ethnically diverse population and to move slightly toward greater gender balance. By 1920, three years after the Calofs left, Ramsey County was almost half female and a quarter foreign-born.[17]

The sheer variety of her neighbors testifies that Rachel Bella Calof was not particularly atypical as an immigrant woman homesteader. It would be hard to choose an average spokesperson for people of such varied origins. The interpretive task is more complex—to sift out what was common in their particular experiences. What adaptations served people who arrived, from different routes, in a common place? What linked their histories and separated their possibilities?

Plainswomen's narratives record some common themes. Many chronicled their struggles learning to keep house in the small soddies, dugouts, or poorly insulated claim shanties of the early settlement period. They wrote of their initial repugnance at having to cook and heat with the dried buffalo or cow dung that was the most abundant fuel in a land with little firewood. They abandoned, of necessity, prior assumptions about appropriate female work, dress, and behavior. Rachel Bella Calof's horror at the "indecent" clothing of "common peasants," the cramped quarters of her "miserable shack," the animal waste on the floor, the inadequate food, and the "terrible crowding" all resonate with other women's words.[18]

So do the details of her arranged marriage, which was not particularly odd in contemporary Jewish practice. "Picture brides" came to the West from many countries, particularly from China and Japan, after single Chinese and Japanese women were restricted from entering the United States. The practice was widespread, however, as immigrant bachelors brought brides from their homelands. Canada recruited immigrant women as domestic servants, hoping they would marry male settlers and stay to establish families and communities in the Canadian West.[19] These common patterns held individual meanings for each woman, depending on particular circumstances and personalities. For some women, arranged marriages were satisfying partnerships. For others, isolated and dependent on strangers, they were frightening and oppressive unions.

In the United States, as in Canada, the state promoted family settlement. Federal land policies were rooted in twin commitments to private property and the nuclear family. The government gave vast acres of public domain to homesteaders and to railroads. The Homestead Act and related laws assumed that most settlers would work their land in family units, and that men would head most families. These arrangements seemed so "normal" to policymakers that other possibilities were hardly imagined. Alternatives might, theoretically, have included collective farms, publicly owned railroads, landholdings worked collectively by extended kin, or communal villages with private gardens and collective grazing land.

There were still some notable exceptions to the nuclear family ideal.

Racist immigration policies denied families to many Chinese and Japanese men.[20] And women could, if they were unmarried or heads of households, claim homesteads on the same terms as men. All the evidence so far indicates that women homesteaders were as successful as men in achieving title to their claims. Always a significant presence on the agricultural frontier, their numbers increased over time, ranging from around 5 percent of all homesteaders in early settlements to some 20 percent after 1900. Few women homesteaders, however, rejected the family model. Many postponed marriage until after they secured title to their land and wed somewhat later than their peers. Others, like Rachel Bella Calof, filed soon before they married, to increase total family holdings, or, as daughters, contributed their land to extended family enterprises.[21]

Women's land ownership did not automatically obliterate existing power relationships between the sexes. Rachel Bella Calof could not, despite her homestead claim, influence basic family decisions—who would live in her house, who would work for wages to support the extended family. Her exclusion from the male family council qualifies easy historical assumptions that land alone empowered women or empowered all women equally. But her obvious resentment also qualifies romantic assumptions about happy, supportive, subordinate wives.

Land ownership increased some women's options and autonomy. For some women, the land provided a "stake" to pursue other dreams, like education or small businesses, or gave them a way to leave.[22] For Rachel Bella and Abraham Calof, more land meant a better chance to survive. In the early years of their marriage, they combined their joint holdings with those of Abe's parents and his brothers. Their two homestead claims did not provide an independent livelihood or, for Rachel Bella, privacy, personal space, or control of her household. Exploring how different men and women allocated work and power, how family and kin were reconfigured in the common terrain of agricultural homesteads, we can learn a great deal about how cultural practices and state policies came together to forge new relationships of gender, power, and possibility for people of different heritages.

One useful contrast comes from the interplay between land policies and the gender relations of the nearby Indians whom Rachel Bella Calof mentions briefly. The Calofs' "free" homesteads rested on the government's ability to restrict the territorial claims of local Indians. The Devils Lake Sioux Reservation, near the Calof homesteads, was established in 1867 through a treaty between the United States and a number of Sioux (Dakota) who settled there, including Sisseton and Wahpeton forced by white settlers from their Minnesota homelands and the Yanktonnai from eastern Dakota Territory. In the late nineteenth century they were joined by Chippewa, technically enrolled on the Turtle Mountain Reservation in north central North Dakota, who were assigned lands next to the Dakota.[23]

The economies, kin relations, and gender roles of these peoples all changed during the reservation period, as the same commitments to private property and family farms enacted in homestead legislation also shaped U.S. Indian policy. The Dawes Act of 1887, which governed Indian relations until the New Deal, severed tribal lands and assigned homesteads to individual nuclear families. Private family farms, it was assumed, would help "raise" and "civilize" Indians. This civilizing mission included "appropriate" gender roles. Government employees and missionaries worked to reverse a traditional Sioux division of labor in crop production, in which women planted and harvested. In the early reservation period, the government gave Sioux men agricultural equipment, stock, and seeds as well as title to family landholdings, effectively excluding Sioux women from agriculture. The women still kept gardens, where they grew root crops, corn, squash, and beans, and they foraged for a variety of fruits, vegetables, and medicinal plants.[24]

Within several decades after the reservation was established, much of the land was lost to railroads. Much more land was alienated under the Dawes Act, which provided that any tribal lands left after individual allotments were distributed would become part of the public domain and sold to railroads and settlers. Much of the land held by Indian men was lost by 1892. During the late nineteenth century, the federal government provided a variety of wage work for the Sioux. The men cut timber, performed janitorial work, and provided other menial labor; the women were taught a variety of domestic skills to use in their own homes or as paid domestic workers.[25]

Federal policies that supported family farms and nuclear families thus held very different meanings for Rachel Bella Calof and her Dakota neighbors. For the Sioux women, the "opportunity" to homestead private family farms engendered considerable loss of status. Their disrupted kin relations became less egalitarian. They lost autonomy and independence as men came to control family land and wages. The Devils Lake Sioux as a whole became increasingly dependent on whites for their survival, and the women's greatest power losses occurred in negotiations between their communities and the government.[26] In contrast, Rachel Bella Calof gained autonomy as she and Abe became more independent of his family. The Calofs' shift from an extended family economy to a separate nuclear family farm increased her sense of power and her ability to control daily household decisions.

The parallel fortunes of Jews and Sioux in North Dakota sketch some of the connected relationships of power, work, kinship, and gender that linked the histories of different groups. One commonality was the difference between the state's ethnic categories and more internal definitions of culture and personal identity. In the terms of the federal laws that governed them, Rachel Bella Calof was white and Russian, the women of the Devils Lake Sioux reservation were Indians, and they were all, presumably, subordinate to men. For the women themselves, other cultural distinctions mattered—whether they were Sisseton, Yanktonnai, or Turtle Mountain Chippewa, Germans from Russia, or Russian or German Jews.

Moreover, factors other than race, ethnicity, and religion could be equally salient for a woman's status and her options—her age, family status, marital status, and what these all meant. How did her people interpret marriage, divorce, widowhood, motherhood, female sexuality? Was she a child, an elder, a wise woman, a healer? These and many other sources of personal identity, as well as many acts of individual resistance, all influenced the relationships of women to their families, to their communities, and to the land.

The ethnic categories of the census do not define the Calofs' cultural context, in which religion figured more significantly than country of origin. The Calofs shared less, for instance, with the more numerous Germans from Russia than they did with Jews from other countries. At the same time, prejudices about national origin, class, and education also divided Jews, and gender differentiated the religious practices, obligations, and statuses of women and men.

The differences between the government's ethnic categories and individual identities bring us to the slippery concept of ethnic culture. Ethnicity itself, like gender, is historically and socially constructed. The concept of ethnic difference arose in heterogeneous societies with organized governments, which labeled particular groups, from within or without, as somehow different from the majority. From the perspective of the state, the labels create important ethnic categories. For the people behind the labels, what they are called may have little to do with their identities, except insofar as official ethnic designations differentiate their rights from the rights of others. Cultures in this sense are a broad range of mental resources and templates that inform identity. They do not rigidly determine behavior, nor are they static or unchanging. Families transmit culture and transform it through daily practice.[27]

This brings us to the intertwined contexts of cultures and the particular people who transmit them. Rachel Bella Calof records how her family adapted Jewish practices to the new contingencies of North Dakota. The Calofs attempted to keep kosher, to perform important life-cycle ceremonies, to celebrate the Jewish holidays. But from the outset Abraham Calof violated the Sabbath when he worked for wages on nearby farms. Rachel Bella hints that, rather than go hungry, they ate pickled pigs' feet they mistakenly bought as herring. She writes that her mother-in-law offered her noodles, chicken, and milk after the birth of her first child, a memory, if accurate, of a violation of the fundamental dietary prohibition against mixing meat and milk.

To read her text as a story of cultural adaptation, we must recognize that the particular cultural traditions she records, which touched her deeply, did not always conform to prescribed Jewish practice. As a woman she was untrained in Jewish law; as an orphan she lacked maternal support. She was isolated by language, by geography, and by her status as a newcomer in the extended Calof family. We cannot know what knowledge of Jewish customs she brought with her from Russia to North Dakota. From whatever combination of background and circumstances, Rachel Bella Calof accepted some practices that pained her and that were not required by Jewish law. Her experience illustrates, in both benign and difficult details, the textures of culture as daily practice rather than as an indelible guide to uniform behavior. The Calofs worked to maintain customs that represented the core of their Jewish identity, while they reconstructed their "Jewishness" in new circumstances.

Throughout her narrative we hear the tension that surrounded Rachel Bella's relationships with her husband's family, particularly with her mother-in-law, Charadh Myers Calof. Rachel Bella sometimes resented the subordinate relationships of children to parents and women to men. Partly she was frustrated that she was powerless in her own household. Her loss of personal privacy compounded her loss of domestic authority. Within their homes, Jewish women prepared religious holidays and ceremonies and performed religious rituals, like blessing the Sabbath candles. Rachel Bella's triumphant pleasure when she fashioned lights from mud, rags, and butter marked twin victories over domestic chaos and religious deprivation. Her lamps lit the house and also enabled her mother-in-law to kindle the Sabbath lights. The Sabbath preparations— cleaning, baking the traditional loaves, and blessing the candles—were ritual pleasures that confirmed Rachel Bella Calof's position as a married woman in her own home. The power to direct and control her household, as both domestic and religious space, was for her a source of order and identity.[28]

Some of the Jewish "traditions" she recorded, however, also frightened, alienated, and pained her. It is important here to consider the different Jewish practices of particular individuals. The most vivid example is Rachel Bella's postpartum terror, induced by her mother-in-law's stories of baby-snatching devils. We cannot generalize from this singular episode to Jewish beliefs or to Jewish women's culture. Another Jewish woman, Doba Calof, intervened with alternative messages to reassure Rachel Bella Calof and restore her world.

In other instances, family customs rather than individual personalities apparently distorted common Jewish practices. Rachel Bella's account of her own wedding, particularly the extended fast before the ceremony and her prolonged isolation behind a blindfold, are extreme versions of wedding customs. The groom veiled the bride before the wedding, but uncovered her face during the ceremony. (This custom derived from the Biblical account that Jacob was tricked into marrying the veiled Leah rather than his intended bride, her younger sister Rachel.) The insistence that Rachel Bella Calof remain in blindfolded isolation after her wedding distanced her from the feasting, dancing, and celebrating that customarily welcomed the bride to the community of married women.[29]

Similarly, when her mother-in-law refused, because it was the Sabbath, to feed Rachel Bella after her first child was born or to light a fire before sundown, she did not recognize a mitigating exception in Jewish law. If health is endangered, then the higher religious obligation to care for life supersedes the requirements to abstain from work on the Sabbath or to fast on Yom Kippur. The *shochet* (ritual butcher) upheld this law when he ordered Rachel Bella, because she was weak from childbirth, to eat from the ox he had declared was not kosher. It may be that the *shochet* was more schooled in Jewish law than was Charadh Calof. His decision provides one instance of cultural adaptability. While the law prescribes that saving life takes precedence over other laws, individuals have to decide when life is at risk. Jewish immigrants constantly negotiated, as families and as individuals, which practices were malleable, and how practice related to Jewish identity.

Class, culture, place, and gender are all conceptual lenses that variously refract and emphasize aspects of experience that are, in individual lives, inseparable. Rachel Bella Calof would, undeniably, have lived a different life had any of these circumstances been changed. As a man she would have worked more outside, spoken in family councils, been spared the physical toll of constant childbearing. Language barriers compounded her isolation as a rural woman. So did her status as an outsider in the extended Calof clan. Just as her experience would have changed had she spoken English, been a man, a child, or Christian, so too would the angle of vision have shifted from which she saw her life. North Dakota was different from inside a shanty than it appeared from behind a plow or the local banker's desk. The view from inside reshapes histories written from the perspectives of public policy, the nation-state, or the daily lives of western men. Only from the multiple perspectives of all the players can we construct a common past.

Seen in the complexity of all her contexts, Rachel Bella Calof shatters the distortions of romantic myth and partial history. Taken out of context, her life could be reduced to the stereotypical endurance of a stoically oppressed helpmate or the romantic triumph of pioneer wifely fortitude. But that is not how Rachel Bella Calof saw herself. She records equally the grim facts of daily endurance and the occasional pleasures that redeemed it, the ignorance and cruelty and the heroic acts of people she disliked. Neither a romantic nor a pessimist, she gives us, with matter-of-fact realism, the life she found worth living.

The affirmative words she chose for her title echo the common Jewish toast "l'chaim," "to life." Rachel Bella Calof affirmed in daily practice the will to survive, to reproduce, to recreate human society. Those daily acts wrote her history and wrote ours as well.

Notes

Thanks to Rabbi Lynn Gottlieb for her support and assistance, to Jacob Calof for sharing his mother's work, and to Sandy Rikoon, for unfailing generosity.

1. Common stereotypes of white western women were first delineated in Beverly Stoeltje, "A Helpmate for Man Indeed: The Image of the Frontier Woman," *Journal of American Folklore* 88:347 (January–March 1975): 27–31. For challenges to the stereotypes, see Susan Armitage, "Through Women's Eyes: A New View of the West," in *The

Women's West, ed. Susan Armitage and Elizabeth Jameson (Norman: University of Oklahoma Press, 1987), pp. 9–18, and in the same anthology, Elizabeth Jameson, "Women as Workers, Women as Civilizers: True Womanhood in the American West," pp. 145–64.

2. On eastern urban Jews, see Irving Howe and Kenneth Libo, *How We Lived: A Documentary History of Immigrant Jews in America, 1880–1930* (New York: R. Marek, 1979), and *World of Our Fathers* (New York: Harcourt Brace Jovanovich, 1976). For Jewish women, see Susan Anita Glenn, *Daughters of the Shtetl: Jewish Immigrant Women in America's Garment Industry, 1880–1920* (Ithaca: Cornell University Press, 1990); Sydney Stahl Weinberg, *The World of Our Mothers: The Lives of Jewish Immigrant Women* (Chapel Hill: University of North Carolina Press, 1988); and, for a fictional version, Anzia Yezierska, *Bread Givers* (New York: Doubleday, 1925). For Jews in the West, see Kenneth Libo and Irving Howe, *We Lived There, Too: In Their Own Words and Pictures— Pioneer Jews and the Westward Movement of America, 1630–1930* (New York: St. Martin's/ Marek, 1984), and Harriet Rochlin and Fred Rochlin, *Pioneer Jews: New Life in the Far West* (Boston: Houghton Mifflin, 1984).

3. This image is drawn largely from the prescribed roles of upper-class white women delineated in Barbara Welter, "The Cult of True Womanhood: 1820–1860," *American Quarterly* 18:2 (Summer 1966): 151–74. A number of authors questioned the degree to which this ideology described real behavior or applied to western women, women of color, or women workers. See for instance Jameson, "Women as Workers"; Rosalinda Méndez González, "Distinctions in Western Women's Experience: Ethnicity, Class, and Social Change," in Armitage and Jameson, *The Women's West*, pp. 237–52; and Robert L. Griswold, "Anglo Women and Domestic Ideology in the American West in the Nineteenth and Early Twentieth Centuries," in *Western Women: Their Land, Their Lives*, ed. Lillian Schlissel, Vicki Ruíz, and Janice Monk (Albuquerque: University of New Mexico Press, 1988), pp. 15–33.

4. Frederick Jackson Turner, "The Significance of the Frontier in American History," in *Annual Report of the American Historical Association for the Year 1893* (Washington, D.C.: U.S. Government Printing Office, 1894). For revisions of Turner, see Lawrence O. Burnette, Jr., comp., *Wisconsin Witness to Frederick Jackson Turner: A Collection of Essays on the Historian and the Thesis* (Madison: The State Historical Society of Wisconsin, 1961), and Earl Pomeroy, "Toward a Reorientation of Western History: Continuity and Environment," *Mississippi Valley Historical Review* 41:4 (March 1955): 579–600.

5. The new western history is a large, diverse, and vital field, which generates multiple interpretations and considerable internal debate. For representative works, see Patricia Nelson Limerick, *The Legacy of Conquest: The Unbroken Past of the American West* (New York: W. W. Norton, 1987); Richard White, *It's Your Misfortune and None of My Own: A New History of the American West* (Norman: University of Oklahoma Press, 1991); Patricia Nelson Limerick, Clyde A. Milner II, and Charles Rankin, eds., *Trails: Toward a New Western History* (Lawrence: University Press of Kansas, 1991); and William Cronon, George Miles, and Jay Gitlin, eds., *Under an Open Sky* (New York: W. W. Norton, 1992).

6. Western women's history took off following two conferences: the Women's West Conference in Sun Valley, Idaho, August 10–13, 1983, and "Western Women: Their Land, Their Lives," Tucson, Arizona, January 12–15, 1984. Two anthologies resulted: Armitage and Jameson, *The Women's West*, and Schlissel, Ruíz, and Monk, *Western*

Women. For reviews of some of this first wave of scholarship, see Joan M. Jensen and Darlis A. Miller, "The Gentle Tamers Revisited: New Approaches to the History of Women in the American West," *Pacific Historical Review* 49:2 (May 1980): 173–213, and Elizabeth Jameson, "Toward a Multicultural History of Women in the Western United States," *Signs* 13:4 (Summer 1988): 761–91.

7. For a history influenced by the Turnerian framework, see Sandra L. Myres, *Westering Women and the Frontier Experience, 1800–1915* (Albuquerque: University of New Mexico Press, 1982). For the restrictions of private gender relations, see Julie Roy Jeffrey, *Frontier Women: The Trans-Mississippi West, 1840–1880* (New York: Hill & Wang, 1979); for women as reluctant pioneers, see also Lillian Schlissel, *Women's Diaries of the Westward Journey* (New York: Schocken, 1982).

8. The most important work for shaping the direction of the field was Jensen and Miller, "Gentle Tamers Revisited." See also Armitage and Jameson, *The Women's West*; Schlissel, Ruíz, and Monk, *Western Women*; and Jameson, "Toward a Multicultural History." Two useful anthologies are Sucheng Chan, Douglas Henry Daniels, Mario T. García, and Terry P. Wilson, eds., *Peoples of Color in the American West* (Lexington, Mass.: D. C. Heath, 1994), and Vicki L. Ruíz and Ellen Carol Dubois, eds., *Unequal Sisters: A Multicultural Reader in U.S. Women's History*, 2nd ed. (New York: Routledge, 1994).

9. Some of the most fruitful sources were government and church records for such changes in social experience as marriage age and marriage partners, household size, family structure, fertility, mortality, and property ownership. Such data, however, do not reveal subjective experience, for which private literature (letters, diaries, and memoirs) and oral histories have been especially useful sources.

10. Calculated from *Report on Population of the United States at the Eleventh Census: 1890,* pt. 1 (Washington, D.C.: Government Printing Office, 1895), pp. 398–99; *Twelfth Census of the United States: 1900,* pt. 1 (Washington, D.C.: United States Census Office, 1901), pp. 575–608, 736–95.

11. In California, a year after the gold rush, the census counted 123 men for each woman. In Colorado, a year after the Pike's Peak boom, there were 1650 men per hundred women. In the agricultural areas of the Old Northwest and the Plains, the figures were closer. Wisconsin, with 158 men per hundred women in 1840, dropped to a more even 106 or 107 from 1860 to 1930. By 1930, Kansas had the lowest sex ratio of any state west of the Mississippi, with 101 men per hundred women, followed by Texas with 104. Calculated from *Historical Statistics of the United States, Colonial Time to 1970,* bicentennial ed. (Washington, D.C.: U.S. Department of Commerce, 1970), Series A: 195–209. It should be noted, however, that sex ratios are often racially skewed, since census figures do not accurately enumerate Indian women. I am grateful to Heather Kellog for assistance with these figures.

12. See for instance Sylvia Van Kirk, *Many Tender Ties: Women in Fur Trade Society, 1670–1870* (Norman: University of Oklahoma Press, 1983); William R. Swagerty, "Marriage and Settlement Patterns of Rocky Mountain Trappers and Traders," *Western Historical Quarterly* 11:2 (April 1980): 159–80; Jacqueline Peterson and Jennifer S. H. Brown, *The New Peoples: Being and Becoming Metis in North America* (Winnipeg: University of Manitoba Press, 1985); and Antonia I. Castañeda, "Spanish-Mexican Women in the Historiography of Frontier California," *Frontiers* 11:1 (1990): 8–20, and "Presidarias y Pobladoras: Spanish-Mexican Women in Frontier Monterey, Alta California, 1770–1821" (Ph.D. diss., Stanford University, 1990).

13. *U.S. Census, 1890, Population*, pt. 3 (Washington, D.C.: Government Printing Office, 1894), pp. 468–69, 234; Melvin E. Kazek, *North Dakota: A Human and Economic Geography* (Fargo: North Dakota Institute for Regional Studies, North Dakota Agricultural College, 1956), p. 35. For independent women homesteaders in North Dakota, see H. Elaine Lindgren, *Land in Her Own Name: Women Homesteaders in North Dakota* (Fargo: North Dakota Institute for Regional Studies, North Dakota State University, 1991).

14. *1890 Census*, p. 501; *U.S. Census, 1920, Population*, vol. 3 (Washington, D.C.: Government Printing Office, 1921), p. 760.

15. *U.S. Census, 1900, Population*, pt. 1 (Washington, D.C.: United States Census Office, 1901), p. 596. Of North Dakotans, 24,257 had Russian-born fathers; 24,445 had Russian-born mothers. Forty percent of all immigrants and 43 percent of North Dakotans were women (*1900 Census*, p. 596). By 1910, Ramsey County was 43 percent female, 31 percent foreign-born, and 39 percent second-generation immigrant. *U.S. Census, 1910, Population*, vol. 3 (Washington, D.C.: Government Printing Office, 1913), pp. 355, 596, 20.

16. *1910 Census*, p. 333.

17. *1920 Census*, pp. 764, 760. In 1920, 425 Russians, 507 Canadians, and 1,121 Norwegians were enumerated on the Ramsey County census. The population was 47 percent female and 26 percent immigrant.

18. This is not to suggest that all women were so miserable. Life cycle seems particularly to have affected women's responses to the early settlement period, which single women and children appear to recall, understandably, with greater fondness and sense of adventure than did married women of childbearing age, for whom the domestic challenges were more burdensome.

19. See Sucheng Chan, ed., *Entry Denied* (Philadelphia: Temple University Press, 1991), esp. Chan, "The Exclusion of Chinese Women, 1870–1943," pp. 94–146; see also Yuji Ichioka, "*Amerika Nadeshiko*: Japanese Immigrant Women in the United States, 1900–1924," *Pacific Historical Review* 49:2 (1980): 339–57. For a grim account of a Swiss picture bride, see Mari Sandoz's autobiographical novel *Old Jules* (Lincoln: University of Nebraska Press, 1962); on Canada, see Norma J. Milton, "Essential Servants: Immigrant Domestics on the Canadian Prairies, 1885–1930," in Armitage and Jameson, *The Women's West*, pp. 207–18.

20. See Chan, *Entry Denied*.

21. See Sheryll Patterson-Black, "Women Homesteaders on the Great Plains Frontier," *Frontiers* 1:2 (Spring 1976): 67–88; Paula Nelson, "No Place for Clinging Vines: Women Homesteaders on the South Dakota Frontier" (M.A. thesis, University of South Dakota, 1978); Lindgren, *Land in Her Own Name*; and Katherine Harris, *Long Vistas: Women and Families on Colorado Homesteads* (Niwot, Colo.: University Press of Colorado, 1993).

22. Lindgren, *Land in Her Own Name*, pp. 189–208.

23. Patricia C. Albers, "Sioux Women in Transition: A Study of Their Changing Status in Domestic and Capitalist Sectors of Production," in *The Hidden Half: Studies of Plains Indian Women*, ed. Patricia Albers and Beatrice Medicine (Latham, Md.: University Press of America, 1983), pp. 175–236, esp. pp. 180–81. Other articles in this anthology are also useful for understanding changing gender roles of Plains Indian women. See also

Patricia Albers, "The Regional System of the Devils Lake Sioux," (Ph.D. diss., University of Wisconsin–Madison, 1974).

24. Albers, "Sioux Women in Transition," pp. 182–94. Sioux women's status decline was by no means simple or complete. Women in the early reservation period, for instance, sold garden produce and other domestic commodities and retained some control through their power to divorce. As with the Calofs, the Sioux began by combining their land into farms managed by extended kin, while the government continued to push for nuclear family operations.

25. Ibid., pp. 194, 186.

26. Ibid., pp. 192–93. This is a brief summary of a subtle analysis that explores subsequent changes in gender relations to 1972.

27. This is a highly condensed discussion of a complex body of theory. For contested theories of culture, see Clifford Geertz, *The Interpretation of Culture* (New York: Basic Books, 1973), and James Clifford, *The Predicament of Culture: Twentieth Century Ethnography, Literature and Art* (Cambridge: Harvard University Press, 1988). For a useful critique, see Peggy Pascoe, "Introduction: The Challenge of Writing Multicultural Women's History," and "Race, Gender, and Intercultural Relations: The Case of Interracial Marriage," *Frontiers* 12:1 (1991): 1–4, 5–18. This discussion draws particularly from Micaela di Leonoardo, *The Varieties of Ethnic Experience: Kinship, Class, and Gender among California Italian-Americans* (Ithaca: Cornell University Press, 1984), esp. pp. 22–24.

28. See Weinberg, *World of Our Mothers*; Glenn, *Daughters of the Shtetl*; and Judith Reesa Baskin, *Jewish Women in Historical Perspective* (Detroit: Wayne State University Press, 1991). On women's religious practices, see Ellen Umansky and Dianne Ashton, *Four Centuries of Jewish Women's Spirituality: A Sourcebook* (Boston: Beacon, 1992); on Jewish women's prayers (*tkhines*), see Tracey Guren Klirs, ed., *The Merit of Our Mothers: A Bilingual Anthology of Jewish Women's Prayers* (Cincinnati: Hebrew Union College Press, 1992). See also Susannah Heschel, *Women in Judaism* (New York: Schocken, 1983); Judith Plaskow, *Standing Again at Sinai: Judaism from a Feminist Perspective* (San Francisco: Harper San Francisco, 1990); and Lynn Gottlieb, *She Who Dwells Within: A Feminist Vision of a Renewed Judaism* (San Francisco: HarperCollins, 1995). For an interesting comparison to Rachel Bella Calof's experience, see Sophie Trupin, *Dakota Diaspora: Memoirs of a Jewish Homesteader* (Lincoln: University of Nebraska Press, 1984).

29. I am grateful to Rabbi Lynn Gottlieb for helping distinguish Jewish law and custom from particular practices.

INDEX

Jacob Calof, the last of Rachel Bella and Abraham Calof's nine children, was born in Devils Lake, North Dakota, in 1912. He now lives in Bellevue, Washington.

Elizabeth Jameson, Associate Professor of History at the University of New Mexico, is co-editor of *The Women's West*. She is the author of articles on western women's history, and was a co-founder of the Coalition for Western Women's History.

J. Sanford Rikoon is Research Associate Professor in the Department of Rural Sociology at the University of Missouri-Columbia. He is the author of *Threshing in the Midwest, 1820–1940*.

CPSIA information can be obtained at www.ICGtesting.com
Printed in the USA
LVOW11s1726310714

396938LV00004B/662/P